'This book should be essential reading fo: [barcode] works with children and young people. It reading for anyone working or interested in the fields of equality and diversity. Anna's writing style draws the reader in to some very personal stories and anecdotes and acts as a useful how to guide to support children and young people questioning their gender identity. The book challenges the reader to go on a deep dive to explore their own thoughts, feelings and unconscious prejudices. The book is also structured as a workbook to support parents and carers of children and young people, guiding them on a journey to being truly inclusive parents. Written at a time of challenging debate around gender identity and the rights of transgender people, I cannot recommend this book enough.'

– Berkeley Wilde, Director, The Diversity Trust

'Anna Bianchi, in her empathy and wisdom as a grandmother and a scholar, goes deep and wide, from our insides to the outside world, guiding us on the journey of building a circle of support around our gender creative children, whether they be our grandchild, our own child, or every child. With gender-expansive children as our leaders, Bianchi teaches us how to achieve the acceptance, advocacy and activism that qualify us as allies to the children. A must-read.'

– Diane Ehrensaft, Ph.D., Director of Mental Health,
Child and Adolescent Gender Center and author of The Gender
Creative Child *and* Gender Born, Gender Made

'As a young trans person who is currently transitioning, I feel that books like this are vital in helping people support and understand those in the trans community.'

– Nia

'In this powerful offering, the author weaves a combination of biography and parental advice into the important topics of safety, labels, bigotry and forgiveness. Enthusiastically recommended for growing collections on transgender youth.'

– Library Journal starred review

of related interest

He's Always Been My Son
A Mother's Story about Raising Her Transgender Son
Janna Barkin
ISBN 978 1 78592 747 8
eISBN 978 1 78450 525 7

The Gender Agenda
A First-Hand Account of How Girls and Boys Are Treated Differently
Ros Ball and James Millar
Foreword by Marianne Grabrucker
ISBN 978 1 78592 320 3
eISBN 978 1 78450 633 9

Straight Expectations
The Story of a Family in Transition
Peggy Cryden, LMFT
ISBN 978 1 78592 748 5
eISBN 978 1 78450 537 0

How to Understand Your Gender
A Practical Guide for Exploring Who You Are
Alex Iantaffi and Meg-John Barker
Foreword by S. Bear Bergman
ISBN 978 1 78592 746 1
eISBN 978 1 78450 517 2

Can I tell you about Gender Diversity?
A guide for friends, family and professionals
CJ Atkinson, illustrated by Olly Pike
ISBN 978 1 78592 105 6
eISBN 978 1 78450 367 3

Who Are You?
The Kid's Guide to Gender Identity
Brook Pessin-Whedbee
Illustrated by Naomi Bardoff
ISBN 978 1 78592 728 7
eISBN 978 1 78450 580 6

BECOMING AN ALLY TO THE GENDER-EXPANSIVE CHILD

A Guide for Parents and Carers

Anna Bianchi

Jessica Kingsley *Publishers*
London and Philadelphia

First published in 2018
by Jessica Kingsley Publishers
73 Collier Street
London N1 9BE, UK
and
400 Market Street, Suite 400
Philadelphia, PA 19106, USA

www.jkp.com

Library of Congress Cataloging in Publication Data
A CIP catalog record for this book is available from the Library of Congress

British Library Cataloguing in Publication Data
A CIP catalogue record for this book is available from the British Library

ISBN 978 1 78592 051 6
eISBN 978 1 78450 305 5

Printed and bound in Great Britain

CONTENTS

AUTHOR'S NOTE

Every family culture is different and, for some readers, the culture they are living in will be different from the one they were born into. It's not within my gift to address the rich complexities of these layers. However, irrespective of cultural variables, all children are trained to fit into the society they are growing up in. The gender binary of male or female is vigorously upheld across the world, even if these roles look distinctive in each region of it.

Our identities are pieced together as a mosaic, not as a straight line. Gender is only one aspect of this. All the parts we embody interact and influence each other. For some people, this means their lives are both nurtured by multiple differences and targeted more because of them. It's a matter of importance to me to acknowledge this from the outset, even though fully exploring 'intersectional'[1] identities is beyond the scope of this book.

I also want to acknowledge the limits of my own experience as someone who is cisgender and expresses myself, predominantly, in ways that are socially typical. I am an ally, and I don't profess to be an expert on anyone's experience other than my own. I can only talk for

---

1   See the interview – Adewunmi, B. (2014) 'Kimberlé Crenshaw on intersectionality: "I wanted to come up with an everyday metaphor that anyone could use."' *New Statesman*, 2 April 2014. Available at www.newstatesman.com/lifestyle/2014/04/kimberl-crenshaw-intersectionality-i-wanted-come-everyday-metaphor-anyone-could, accessed on 14 July 2017.

myself and not for anyone else. Endeavouring to listen and, eventually, to listen deeply enough to other people, revealed this truth to me in the first place.

Finally, I began writing this book from a position of 'not knowing' – not knowing much about gender identity beyond the binary of male/female, man/woman. I finished it in a position of deep humility. I bow the knee to my teachers: children and adults, past and present, of all sexes and genders. I had not made it my business before to educate myself about your vibrant communities. I had no idea of the sustained attacks, and anguish, you've survived for so long. For this, I offer you an apology. My grandchild is safer because of your struggles. For this, I offer you thanks.

It's the whole child-led thing isn't it, which sounds hippy and leftie, but it's person-led, not child-led – listening to someone else before you make a decision about their care for them. You want to give them every chance to express themselves. I'm sure it's the same for every parent and child, isn't it? Give your child a chance to express themselves. Then when they show you who they are, celebrate it.

Father of a seven-year-old transgender girl

INTRODUCTION

I had no premonition, when my first grandchild was born, that I would be writing this book. How could I know that Ruben's birth would lead me to question many of my essential 'truths' about being male or female? That his small fierce journey across the landscape of gender would take me on one of my own? That Ruben's insistence on living his own truth would inspire me to live mine more fully? None of us knew then that my grandson, soon to be celebrated in every hue of blue, would undo our gender bearings. These were impossible circumstances to imagine the morning Ruben arrived. I simply held him to my heart and gazed into his face, as surely in-love as I've ever been in the whole of my life.

By the time our boy was three his preference for toys, games, clothes and activities began to all go against the gender grain. At first it was subtle, choosing a pink lunch box, wanting to wear slides in his hair, refusing to wear a navy dressing gown. Six months or so later, Ruben seemed to have crossed over some internal divide and, to our great consternation, began to declare his identity as a girl. At four, Ruben's clarity about his own gender path was apparent to anyone that knew him. As two extended families, joined together in one child, we didn't approach this unknown path recklessly. Indeed, every decision was significant, and all of them were weighed with care: first, against Ruben's overall welfare, and second, against our own bias and potential prejudice.[1] These conflicting components were far from easy to untangle, yet unconditional love always motivated us to attempt to do so.

Over the months, as my grandchild trusted the inner thermal that carried him towards an emerging reality, I often struggled. My fears, my politics, my prejudice, my assumptions and attitudes were all exposed, caught up, spun around and scattered by this experience. And time and time again, they were transformed and grounded in the simple truth of Ruben's commitment to living authentically. There is something both tender and terrifying in witnessing a child you love breaking gender rules they're just beginning to learn. As Ruben began to traverse the territory between his assigned gender and his felt gender, I often held my breath. When he went through the school gates, wearing a girl's cardigan with a scalloped collar, or black leggings instead of boy's trousers, even at five he did so with awareness. Ruben wasn't making a political point, seeking attention or trying to prove something, he was simply being himself as he understood himself to be. His radical innocence and the faith he showed to manifest it, undid me.

About this time, I wrote a blog post about my experience and the journey of acceptance it had initiated me into. Unbeknown to me, it was passed on to an editor of a national newspaper in the United Kingdom, who subsequently approached me to write an article for the family section of *The Telegraph*. Its publication elicited a small storm of attention in my life, which I found deeply disconcerting. Then a close relative expressed to me her reserve that I'd written about my grandchild, without his permission. I chose to sit in the fire of her loving feedback and not turn away from the tumultuous feelings it provoked in me. This was a vital thing to do. I finally fell asleep that

---

1   A bias is a tendency to look at things a certain way in preference to others, and prejudice is a preconceived mind-set that obscures the impartial judgement of ideas or people. The difference between the two states is an important one.

night with those feelings still drumming in my chest. When I woke the following morning, they had gone and an all-consuming knowing had taken their place: *I don't have time to wait for the world to change. Ruben is five already. I need to do everything in my power to change the world for him and for all children like him.*

In the wake of my grandchild's choices, I chose to wrestle with myself rather than automatically impose a fixed reality onto him. In doing so, I stood down from being the all-knowing adult and became an apprentice to life instead. This shift in perception meant I let go of expectations and opened up to the experience in front of me. It was against this backdrop that I then received an invitation from Jessica Kingsley Publishers to submit a book proposal to them. I was quite overwhelmed for a few days after their offer. I'm cisgender and, not only that, I've always expressed my gender in fairly typical ways. What useful contribution could I make? And, more pertinently, what was I actually qualified to write about? I remember walking in a park close to my home around this time, contemplating the answer. Autumn had taken hold and the remaining flowers were folding themselves back into the earth. I paced the well-worn path, purposely shifting my attention from my head to my heart, listening for any guidance within myself. When it came, it was precise: *You're asking the wrong question, Anna. The right question is this one: What's the book that wants to get written through you?* By the time I'd returned home, grabbed some paper and begun to scribble, another urgent question had arisen in me: *How best can parents and caregivers accept and protect their gender-expansive child?* The answer is the heart of my own personal story as a grandmother, and of this book: by choosing to become an ally. To successfully accomplish this we have to break open our understanding of what gender is. To do so means to embark on our own private inner journey, side-by-side with our child on their outer one.

The path of an ally

It takes courage to challenge oneself – to deliberately set out on a passage of self-discovery with no promise of comfort; to set out, in fact, anticipating effort and endurance, confusing terrain, steep gradients and a dwindling sense of certainty. The motivation for embarking on such a journey in the first place must be compelling. And the reason for doing so big enough to overcome any fear it provokes. For many of you turning these pages now, that reason is to do with love. You may be a parent who fears the wrong decision could devastate your child's social or emotional well-being; a foster-carer who thinks gender-expansive behaviour is 'bad' and you're now conflicted about your role, or a grandparent who's embarrassed by your granddaughter's preferences and feels guilt over this. I believe you want what is best for your child and, like the rest of us, find yourself caught in the complex pattern of your own gender perspective, prejudice and history. In effect, your child's outer journey has already initiated an inner one for you. More often than not, this parallel process is ignored by others, despite it being integral to what's happening in your family. This can lead to increased anxiety, growing inhibitions and feelings of isolation for everyone involved. If this situation continues unresolved, your child is in danger of becoming trapped between the conflicting forces, unspoken fears and unconscious actions of the adults around them.

This book is concerned with building the capacity of you as parents and caregivers to engage with your child's process, and your own. The two are inseparable. This is the terrain we need to march towards and map out. As we shall discover, society has trained us to be enemies, not allies, to people who express gender differently from the mainstream. Adults who choose to travel into, rather than turn away from this territory, deserve support. And though it may feel lonely at times, please hold onto this truth: courage arises from your willingness to prioritise your child's needs above all others. Taking full ownership for your own feelings, and protecting your child from those who are unprepared to do this for themselves, establishes you as a leader. You are a change-maker, even if you don't seek this accolade or wish it upon yourself at all.

What you need to remember

When we challenge our assumptions, attitudes and beliefs, we're taking the road less travelled. To do this in the context of parenting and caregiving, even more so. For most of us the stakes can't get any higher. I want to acknowledge that there may well be some uncomfortable, and even scary, times ahead. Given this, there's a vital aspect of our work together that I need to mention specifically: self-care. Self-care means what it says on the tin. It includes any intentional actions that support your physical, emotional, spiritual and mental health. Take a moment now and ask yourself what helps your body and mind to feel good? It might be meditation, an art class, a spa day, sitting under a tree, marathon running, a bike ride or spending time with animals. Your life history, present circumstances and support network will all influence what serves to relax and energise you. Self-care isn't a luxury, it's a strategy to assist you in supporting your child – as much a strategy as reading this book, calling a helpline or researching gender diversity online. Please give it some serious consideration before we set out. It's a major piece of kit in your backpack for the journey ahead.

The second critical thing you need to bring to this process is willingness. The usefulness of this book hinges on your willingness to use 'reflective thinking'. By this I mean exercising your ability to reflect on your attitudes, values and behaviour. This means cultivating the capacity to 'step back' inside yourself and to think and feel through your experiences honestly. It'll mean asking some searching questions of yourself, practising being 'open' and promising not to 'hide' behind any well-rehearsed defences. Many of us find reflective thinking difficult to do on a regular basis, especially where conflict is involved. I want to encourage you to commit to this practice because I'm confident it will bring its own rewards. As you do so, it will illuminate your reactive thinking and behaviour, alleviate painful feelings such as regret and enable you to make conscious, healthier choices for your child. It also has the power to transform your relationship with yourself. This last point is a very important one. Taking responsibility for your process, your own journey, is empowering. You know yourself, your child and your circumstances best. It's a daunting and exciting choice to create a gender-healthy environment in your home, one in which your child will thrive, irrespective of future challenges.

It's also important that I state clearly what this book isn't. This book isn't a parenting manual, designed to teach you how to care for your child, though it may indeed influence your existing parenting style. Nor is it a conclusive take on a highly complex subject. As caregivers, we must all learn to let go of expectations and stay open to experience. There are very few simple equations. And it may be a long time before 'answers' are arrived at. My family, like yours, is living this process stage by stage, trusting that each new threshold will bring with it what we need.

From mother to grandmother...

When I look back 30 years, I see myself as a young inexperienced mum with another gender-expansive little one: my first child Adam, when he was seven. Adam loathed the monotony of boy's clothes and longed for the rainbow colours available to his sister. As he got older, I spent hours searching for attire that was 'boy enough' to keep him from being teased and 'girl enough' to satisfy his need for something beautiful. I rarely, if ever, succeeded in my quest. And while Adam expressed his gender identity in flamboyant and feminine ways at home, we strongly influenced him to subdue his impulses in public – partly because his father and I didn't process fully what was happening, and partly because we wanted to shield him from judgement and criticism.[2] Sometimes it intruded on our son's innocence anyway. I remember, one occasion, when Adam was playing with David, a neighbour's child. The two boys had been happily preoccupied all afternoon dressing Adam's collection of Barbie dolls and making new clothes for them. As his friend left to return home, I was touched when Adam offered to lend him one of his precious dolls. David was delighted although his shy pleasure was short-lived. Within ten minutes he was back clutching the Barbie in his outstretched hand, eyes cast down and cheeks inflamed: 'My dad won't let me keep it. He told me to give it back straight away.' There, right on my doorstep, I understood how gender norms and the baton of homophobia are forced into a boy's hand and bound there with shame and the terror of rejection – gender-expansive or not.

Now I have another seven-year-old at the centre of my life – one who has taken me beyond the milestones that Adam and I encountered together – far beyond them. Ruben has now socially transitioned to Ruby and lives fully as a girl. She is happy. Throughout the book I'll use the name Ruben to refer to my grandchild prior to transition and use Ruby after transition. This makes for clarity when I'm recounting elements of my story, and it also honours the process my grandchild is in.[3] You'll also meet some other children, young people and their family members in the following pages.

---

2   Many years later, when I spoke to Adam's dad and revealed to him that our son was gay, his response bonded me to him forever, despite the fact that our marriage eventually ended. We were away for the weekend and eating dinner in a restaurant. I recall how he first placed his knife and fork down, then took a breath, looked at me and said, 'You know I don't understand this. But he's my son and I love him. That's all there is to it.' And so it was.

3   Ruby, at present, is completely at ease with her history as Ruben. She's comfortable with looking at photos and still plays happily with certain toys that she had when she was a toddler. Her experience, of course, is an individual one and, in no way, represents every child's.

Their names and any identifying details have been changed to ensure confidentiality. I've had the great privilege of meeting many of these contributors in person. All of them have been absolutely fundamental to my learning.

I've chosen to use the term 'gender-expansive' to refer to all children who don't conform to their culture's expectations for boys or girls. Being transgender is one way of being gender-expansive, but not all gender-expansive children are transgender. There are many variables. This is an important distinction to hold in mind. Where I use 'transgender', I'm specifically referring to someone whose gender identity doesn't match the biological sex they were assigned at birth; for example, a transgender child who self-identifies as a boy but is biologically female, or vice-versa. It's also important to note that some children and young people self-identify as non-binary and/or trans, meaning their gender doesn't fit neatly into either category.[4]

The journey our exceptional children[5] have initiated us into has brought us together. I'm glad. We need each other's strength and we need each other's company. The book you're now holding in your hands is a physical manifestation of my own initiation so far. Your journey is of equal value and potential and arises out of the uniqueness of your circumstances. Who knows what we can achieve together? What matters is that we work collectively to generate rapid social change, so all children one day will be equally welcomed and safe.

---

4   I'm aware that language is slippery and these terms vary according to their context and source. Some young people reject the term 'trans' as an identity, and others embrace it. Terminology referring to a range of gender identities has never been more sophisticated. I will go on to discuss this later in the book.

5   I borrow this term from Andrew Solomon: Solomon, A. (2014) *Far from the Tree: Parents, Children, and the Search for Identity*. London: Penguin Random House.

The 'Gender Matrix'

We have been taught that gender is locked, enduring and only exists as two categories. Every person on the planet must fit into the one they were assigned to at birth, or face the consequences of not doing so. This is what I call the Gender Matrix, a gender system, based on the sovereignty of the binary, male or female, which dictates identity and demands allegiance. To become an ally means opposing the Gender Matrix and we shall soon discover the enormity of this undertaking. It's a persuasive and pervasive system that leaves no part of our life untouched. As such, it's also a binding force in the psyches of most human beings. The overwhelming majority of people in the world are 'cisgender', that is, they identify with the gender assigned to them at birth and, significantly, they're heterosexual too. This makes for majority rule. A matrix, typically, is defined as a set of conditions in which something grows and develops. Geologists use the term to describe rock as the matrix on which gems, fossils and crystals eventually become embedded. The binary forms the social rock in which ideas, norms, rules, expectations, opinions and attitudes about gender synthesise and fuse together. Collectively, they solidify into what we know as 'mainstream culture', which is founded on the premise that to be cisgender and heterosexual is to be 'normal'. Non-mainstream groups, from their position on the outside, recognise and refer to this embedded bias as 'heteronormative'. As a result of this, the degree of gender conditioning that has moulded each one of us is incalculable. Consequently, we internalise a palette of beliefs, taboos, biases, stereotypes, assumptions and prejudices associated with gender and sexuality. We haven't consciously chosen these and we may not even want them. Nevertheless, they form the bricks and mortar that keep the structure upright. Unbeknown to us, we gradually inhabit the Matrix and become its subjects without our informed consent. And this, in turn, impacts on the gender journeys of the children we're responsible for.

Our gender-expansive little ones, in their radical innocence, are unaware of this. They walk onto the stage of life guided by their inner vision, free of any gender cataracts. They have no idea that they're confronting one of the most powerful convictions of human experience. It's the reason why children who dress, play and communicate in gender-expansive ways often, without intention, disturb the environment around them. People can rarely say *why* they feel provoked by this behaviour; they just know that they do. Alongside this, such behaviour often triggers an association between gender and sexuality, which, although related, are not the same. This coupling frequently produces complex feelings in us, including unbidden homophobic responses. Because we perceive such feelings as 'threatening', we often push them away and resist exploring them. While this is still the norm, it's easy to see how parents and caregivers often feel stranded with their difficulties, and even ashamed of their own feelings and fears. We may even identify with a community that knows a great deal about the experience of difference, and still, to our dismay, find this particular difference hard to accept.

The Gender Matrix has much in common with the story of rock. Both appear to be a dense and solid mass, yet both evolve over the time. The 'rock cycle', as it's called, comes about when processes on and under the earth, force change. In time, a new physical landscape will emerge that reflects this slow movement and unrelenting momentum. So, too, with us as human beings. External events and internal processes force change as we learn, grow and make sense of our lives. Collectively, this creates cultural shifts that eventually lead to wider societal ones.[6] It's the epic story of humanity, mapped onto the face of time. The many gate-keepers of the Matrix would have us believe otherwise. Their investment is in maintaining a gender

---

6   Changes in ideas and values are a result of multiple influences from different quarters that find a common expression, including academics, writers, social activists, artists, participants on social media and grassroots organisations, youth movements and progressive faith communities.

hierarchy, which is constructed on the binary. If this shaft falls, the entire system goes with it. Many, many gender injustices exist within the Matrix, not least how women and girls remain subject to global discrimination and atrocities because their gender is not a universally empowered one.[7] In writing this specific book, about the need to expand our understanding of gender as a concept, I am in no way minimising or disguising gender-based abuses elsewhere.[8] In addressing the question that runs through it, *'How best can parents and caregivers accept and protect their gender-expansive child?'*, my hope is to link arms across all gender-based oppressions. For me, it took my initiation as a grandmother to teach me what they share in common: each one is rooted in a rejection of anyone who doesn't conform to the binary.

The secrets of the Matrix – how it secures its dominance, exercises control, recruits troops without their permission, manipulates minds and motivates behaviour – exist deep within it. The stone passageways, murky caverns and inner recesses of rock beneath its respectable, 'common sense' façade are our destination. We must tunnel into its foundations and become familiar with them. It's here that we'll find the answers to the questions and dilemmas that trouble us as parents and caregivers who love our gender-expansive children yet struggle, still, with our own unease and prejudice.

We'll begin this campaign with the end always in view: what is an ally, how do you become one, and why are allies essential in the lives of gender-expansive children? We'll identify the 'Four Keys' that we need to become an ally to our child: listening, imagination, empathy and courage. Then we'll take a look at gender identity and the natural inclination children have to follow their own 'Golden Thread' if the

---

7   See the UN Women's report, *Progress of the World's Women 2015–2016*, at http://progress.unwomen.org/en/2015/pdf/UNW_progressreport.pdf, accessed on 14 July 2017.

8   I include in this the suffering of boys and men whose alienation under the Matrix leads to appalling suicide rates across the world.

adults around them permit them to do so. After this, we'll go on to encounter the Matrix within ourselves, understand why we're invested in it, and identify how it is maintained in society, and in our individual psyches. Then we shall unmask it. We'll expose how its central joists are kept in place through the workings of power, privilege and rank, and the monopoly of dominant mainstream language about 'difference', which erases, labels or 'laughs things off'. By now, you'll be able to identify the pattern of interlocking assumptions, attitudes, beliefs and actions that constitute the Matrix in our culture. This will enable you to put your reactions and responses in a larger context. And they will begin to change. You'll see that gender, far from being fixed, is actually a vivid, multidimensional and intriguing spectrum we've been trained to fear.

The second half of the book is a call to action. In it we'll take a conscious shift in our direction and begin to travel inwards. Our focus will be on four inner regions, all of them vital and rich in resources. These chapters will invite you to explore each domain thoroughly and spell out why they're essential to becoming an ally: self-knowledge, self-awareness, self-esteem and self-forgiveness. From here on in there are a number of practical exercises, prompts and activities to generate new learning in you and eradicate outdated material. This process will enable you to acquire knowledge, refine your awareness and re-map what you think and feel about gender, for yourself. In doing so, the Matrix that you inherited will be dismantled, the components sorted and the structure redesigned according to your own expertise. The final two chapters will bring us full circle. We'll explore what 'living as an ally' looks like from this new perspective, and imagine together what 'trusting in the future' means to us, and to our gender-expansive children who have guided us there.

Self-portrait of a trans girl, aged six.

CHAPTER 1

AN INVITATION TO BECOME AN ALLY

Ruben's invitation to me

When we woke, and after I'd told Ruben a Sunday morning story in the hushed house, he went downstairs ahead of me. I followed a few minutes later. Ruben was already dressed, and he'd pulled his basket of toys out from the cupboard under the stairs. He glanced up at me, smiled, and carried on with the business of laying train tracks on my kitchen floor. I remember it was a vivid spring morning and my first-born grandchild held all the promise of it. I put his orange beaker and my cup of tea on the table, and sat down next to him to choose the train I wanted to be. A while later, we were both hungry. I'd promised Ruben pancakes the evening before but then discovered I didn't have any eggs. My suggestions of cereal or toast weren't welcome and his suggestion of going to the nearby shop was persistent. Eventually I conceded. Our conversation, as I recall it now, went something like this,

'Okay, sweetheart, we can go out, but Nanny needs you to get changed.'

'I'm dressed already, Nanny.' Ruben looked down at the clothes he was wearing as if to confirm it. The powder-blue princess gown he had brought with him the evening before, fitted him perfectly. Its silver sleeves travelled snugly all the way down to his wrists.

'I know, but Nanny thinks you might get cold.'

'It's sunny outside.'

We both glanced out of the window. Ruben looked at the blue sky and I looked at the two men walking by, with a dog pulling on a lead. A boy followed just behind them with a football in his hands. I looked down at my grandson. He brushed the shiny surface of his gown as though to comfort it. I picked up my dirty cup and turned to put it into the sink.

'And I'm worried the hem of your gown will get messy, my darling.'

'But, Nanny, it only comes down to the hip on my shoes.'

Ruben's innocent reply threw open the door of my conscience. The grubby sheet I'd draped over my deceit slid away. I fell into the arms of my grandson's innocence. What on earth was I doing? Why was I telling lies to my little one? Why did I care what he went out in? He wasn't even four yet.

Later, after pancakes and playing and putting all the toys away, it was time for a bath. I was running the water and Ruben was perched nearby. Then he jumped down and began to take off his clothes. I took a step towards him.

'Nanny, you do know I'm a girl, don't you?'

I remember feeling my stomach lurch and being utterly disarmed by my grandson's trust, his unflinching enquiry and the clarity in his solemn brown eyes as they studied mine. For a moment in time I stood in the centre of a bridge spanning two different shores, with my thoughts manhandling each other out of the way. I looked in one direction towards the safety of a gender harbour I recognised and understood. Then I followed Ruben's view towards the other shore and a coastline I couldn't read at the distance I was standing from it. Nothing, truly, in my experience had prepared me for this. Not my parenting of four birth children and a step-son; not all the years I worked as a therapeutic social worker with young people or an equalities specialist in different settings. I knew in my bones, as Ruben waited for an answer, I was being confronted with two stark choices: influence my grandchild to deny his own reality or dare myself to redefine my own.

When Ruben held my gaze and waited for my answer to his question, I waited too. I didn't know what I was going to say to him in reply.

'Nanny, you do know I'm a girl, don't you?'

Then, in response, my words: 'Are you, sweetheart? Is that all of the time, or only some of the time?'

'All of the time.'

Ruben and I stood together. I stroked his hair and then put my hand in the bath water to make sure it wasn't too hot.

'Ready, Nanny?' he asked me, leaning forward.

'Almost, my darling, almost.'

Becoming an ally

When Ruben asked me his question that day, others ripped through my awareness as he spoke: 'Why on earth would he think this thing?' 'If I support him, will it harm him?' 'Can this be right?' And then, on a subtler and much more shadowy level: 'What will people think of me if I do take Ruben seriously?' Perhaps some of the thoughts and feelings I had then, resonate with you in your situation now. You may even fear that enabling a child to express their gender identity freely is morally wrong and unacceptable. If you're willing to listen to your heart and, even jump off the edge of it into unexplored places, then bring all these anxieties and misgivings with you too. Fear, discomfort, panic and uncertainty are indispensable steps of this process. Accepting this fact allows you to engage with what's happening and to struggle, rather than resort to fight or flight behaviour. As human beings we find 'not knowing' almost unbearable and will often act prematurely to put an end to it. Go gently with yourself. The tricky thing is to stay with your uncertainty long enough for it to authentically evolve into something else. We need to be patient and resilient as we find our way out of these straits and into clearer water.

Allies who are concerned with social justice are people who align themselves with a person who's been pushed to the edge of a group, or with a group that's been pushed to the edges of society. Embracing and embodying this role takes time – it's a process. Becoming an ally to a gender-expansive child is a decision. You may have made it gradually, or you may have made it all at once. What counts is that you've made it. The process of becoming an ally to your particular child is yours to discover and own. As you move forward, the ground beneath your feet will start to feel steady. This comes about through the choices we make, one by one, along the way. There isn't a definitive 'to-do' list or a programme to complete with a certificate at the end of it. The evidence, always and inevitably, will be in the quality of the relationship you have with your offspring – ultimately, whether they feel able to turn to you for unconditional love and support or must go in search of it elsewhere. So the bedrock of your identity, as an ally, is created both inside and outside of yourself. This may look like you prioritising some 'time out' to be with your feelings or thoughts about what's challenging you. It may look like you squaring up to your own disquiet and gender prejudice. Or it may be apparent in your new-found determination to listen rather than 'talk over' your child. Your personal signature as an ally will reveal itself as the journey progresses – how you fight your child's corner, what you do to educate yourself about their experience, how you educate others and, how the detail of your own internal landscape is beginning to shift. These are both the tiny stitches and the weighted fabric that piece together the canvass you and your child can shelter under together. There will be forward and backward movements, and you must be prepared to forgive yourself when you get something 'wrong' because, inevitably, you will on occasions. Everyone can choose to learn from their errors. An error becomes a mistake only when we refuse to own, apologise and make amends for it where possible. Perfection, thank goodness, is not a prerequisite for becoming an ally.

Safety and risk

One of the heaviest responsibilities any committed parent carries is how to balance safety and risk in relation to their child. When we factor in a difference such as gender nonconformity, risk can feel as though it has the master key to our front door. For many of us, the decision to become an ally is the decision to become an activist. It's the single action that creates the most leverage in safeguarding our child's welfare. Most of you, I'm sure, will be aware of the frightening threats associated with gender diversity. While it's vital we're informed about these, it's also vital that our fear regarding risk doesn't consume us. A new gender story is being written and our children are part of it. We need to hold the breadth of this vision in our hearts, even as we seek to protect our kids and enable them to thrive as who they are.

In 2016, the largest comprehensive study ever devoted to the experience of transgender and gender 'nonconforming'[1] people was published. *The Report of the 2015 U.S. Transgender Survey* captures the experiences of 27,715 respondents.[2] It makes for painful reading. And it also confirms what many of us intuitively know: *a chief safety factor in reducing risk is to belong to an accepting family.* In this circumstance, when immediate family were supportive, the risk of serious psychological distress and self-harm was far less likely than in families that were unsupportive. As a social worker, I learnt quickly in my career that when children were loved for who they were, rather than labelled and rejected for 'what' they were, risk diminished dramatically. The theory on improving resilience in children is now conclusive: when a child can count on even one adult, to hold them

---

1   I'm personally uncomfortable with the term 'nonconforming' because it only makes sense in the context of deviating from what's regarded as 'normal'.
2   National Center for Transgender Equality (2015) *The Report of the 2015 U.S. Transgender Survey.* Available at www.ustranssurvey.org/report, accessed on 14 July 2017.

in 'heart and mind' at all times, the positive impact of this can be astonishing. That adult can be an uncle, a teacher, a foster-carer, a cousin, a neighbour, a grandparent, a mother, a father.[3] The bottom line is this: where there are allies, there's increasing safety; and where allies are absent, there's increasing risk. Allies, in the stories of gender-expansive children, are a lifeline to increased resilience, healthy self-esteem and good decision-making capacities. An ally marks the place of refuge that a child can find their way to, in any set of circumstances.

When we pledge to become an ally, there's a 'why' and a 'how' embedded in our impulse. For us, the why is an expression of unconditional love and acceptance, and a fierce commitment to shield and protect our exceptional child. The how is less clearly defined and is discovered in the doing. The path of the how is found in two places: the external world of society, culture, community and family; and the interior world of our own being. The two paths intertwine as each one influences the other. Our focus is on the inner journey, trusting that what we do here will impact positively on what we do 'out there'. Our mission is to take this path, and to grapple with and discard any brambles, deadwood or rubble that limits our progress on it. The stakes are too high not to. For us, this debris may come in the form of transphobia we don't want, homophobia we're ashamed of, or other outdated and fear-based beliefs. These things are the by-product of living in a social environment polluted by inequality. We all end up absorbing toxicity, simply because we're immersed in it. Acknowledging this reality, and taking action to create an inclusive, healthy 'eco-system' inside yourself, is also the practice of building safety into the life of your child.

---

3   I recommend the work of Angie Hart and her colleagues to you. Their website (www.boingboing.org.uk) is full of practical advice, learning tools and research evidence that all support resilience-building in children. The mantra Angie Hart encourages all adults to use in relation to their child is this: 'What's the next resilient move I can make on their behalf?'

'I know best'

Any adult who commits to being an ally to children must, sooner or later, pay some attention to power and the balance of it within relationships. Both as adults and, in our role as parents and caregivers, we're the ones with all the 'legitimate' power. Granted, a child or young person may try many different ways to control a situation, but let's be clear here: that isn't the same as being imbued with the authority to do so. For many adults, the default position is still 'I know best', simply because we've inherited this perspective from parent figures and had it reinforced culturally. The extent to which this belief is unconscious is the extent to which it will sabotage an alliance with your child.

Adults do not always know best. Most of us have only to look at our own lives to respond to this statement honestly. If we approach our own parenting and caregiving with a good dose of humility and humour, if we listen wholeheartedly to our children, if we're flexible, respectful, consistent where it counts and self-aware *then* we have the grounds to assert our views with some confidence. Adults may bank on authority by virtue of their age, and that isn't the same as earning it by virtue of their wisdom. Getting clear about the power differential between adults and children is non-negotiable when it comes to being an ally. If we remain attached to 'knowing best', then when our children begin to share their internal truth with us we simply won't be able to hear it. I'm not implying here that children and young people always know what's best either. I firmly believe though, that the cultural norm is to pay lip-service to the expertise children and young people have with regard to themselves and their own needs. This is a dangerous precedent. When we ignore what matters to someone personally, and denigrate their direct experience, we are elevating risk whether we choose to acknowledge this or not.

The notion of 'children's rights' is a very recent thing. It wasn't until the twentieth century that children were truly recognised as something other than 'adults in waiting' and something more than the 'property' of their parents. The UN Convention on the Rights of the Child 1989 (UNCRC) is a legally binding international agreement setting out the civil, political, economic, social and cultural rights of every child, regardless of their race, religion or abilities. It comprises 54 articles that cover all aspects of a child's life. These articles are guided by four overarching principles that make all the others possible:

1. non-discrimination
2. best interest of the child
3. right to life, survival and development
4. right to be heard.

Eleanor Roosevelt, in her role as chair of the United Nations Human Rights Commission 40 years previously, made her views explicit about where human rights begin:

> In small places, close to home—so close and so small that they cannot be seen on any maps of the world. Yet they are the world of the individual person; the neighborhood he lives in; the school or college he attends; the factory, farm or office where he works. Such are the places where every man, woman, and child seeks equal justice, equal opportunity, equal dignity without discrimination. Unless these rights have meaning there, they have little meaning anywhere. Without concerted citizen action to uphold them close to home, we shall look in vain for progress in the larger world.[4]

Mrs Roosevelt leaves us no space to hide. In modern-day parlance she is challenging us to 'step up'. If we espouse equality, then we must

4   Eleanor Roosevelt's 'The Great Question' remarks were delivered at the United Nations in New York on 27 March, 1958.

walk our talk, whatever ground we find ourselves standing on. As allies we need to take power, rights and responsibilities into account at all times and in all situations. I'll be saying a lot more about this as we progress through the book.

What are the characteristics of an ally?

Although no fixed requirements exist, there is a set of characteristics all allies share in common, whatever or whoever they're committed to. For us, as allies to gender-expansive children, these attributes embody the brawn we need to take apart the gender conditioning we've been steeped in. I'm setting out a stencil to map your intentions onto, which I trust will be helpful. Return to it as often as is useful. Please think of it as a 'working document', which I've included to guide, not test, you.

- *An ally wants to learn.* The will to educate yourself about someone else's direct, lived experience is the pivotal condition of becoming an ally. If there's no will to do this, there isn't a way forward. No-one can truly know what it's like to be another person. If that person has a difference that you don't share, then even less so. An ally isn't attached to their version of the truth about someone else. Quite the opposite, in fact. Their decision to step into this role will be characterised by a devout desire to learn. Wanting to learn, by definition means bringing all of yourself to the learning process. It means being open to new things, and recognising that old things will, necessarily, have to be let go of to make space for them. This is a demanding process because it will lead to periods of confusion and various levels of uncertainty – at least for a while. This stage on the learning cycle is known as 'conscious incompetence'. In other words, you're at the point where previously comfortable certainties are fading away and a new pattern of knowing hasn't yet emerged. You're now on the challenging territory of 'you don't know what you don't know'. Hang in there, this will change.

- *An ally strives to be self-aware.* This means that you take responsibility for yourself and are prepared to put the work in to achieve the outcome you want. If we minimise, challenge or deny the reality of someone else's lived experience, it's a neon light pointing at our own discomfort and defence. When we strive to be more self-aware, we receive this information as feedback about ourselves and not criticism. Self-awareness and the willingness to learn are the twin foundations underpinning personal growth and change.

- *An ally will work to overcome personal barriers.* This means that when you encounter a barrier to your learning, you won't allow it to bring your progress to a standstill. Any barrier will simply be 'grist to the mill'. It will be the vehicle that expands your understanding, heightens your awareness and drives your commitment to change.

- *An ally will hold themselves accountable.* With or without the approval of others, you'll stand for what you believe is right. Privately and publicly. And while it's true that you're primarily accountable to yourself, remember, none of us can get everything right all of the time.

As allies to children particularly, there are two other characteristics we need to include in our vision:

- *An ally will be child-inclusive.* To be child-inclusive means what the term implies: that you aspire to keep the child within your circle of awareness, holding them in mind and heart, wherever they are. Consequently, you don't allow their experience to become swamped by your feelings or eclipsed by somebody else's. If this happens, you're able to recognise it and 'pull back', to shift the focus away from yourself or others, and to vividly 'see' the child again. The shorthand for this is 'holding the space'. When you hold the space for someone, it means you maintain a boundary between their experience and your own. The two don't merge, so any personal concerns and worries you have don't hijack the interaction. This doesn't mean your feelings and thoughts are invalid, or imply they should be ignored. Certainly not. It simply means safeguarding your child from absorbing and taking responsibility for them, and for you. Meanwhile it's imperative that you seek support that you need for yourself elsewhere.

As with parenting that's based on democratic and/or authoritative principles, a child-inclusive ally shows respect for children as individual, rational beings and this governs your behaviour. You value high levels of nurture, communication and standards that will enable your child to prosper. You reason, negotiate, and compromise to achieve this, rather than impose your will on a situation. As a parent or caregiving ally, being, or learning how to become, child-inclusive is central to achieving the outcomes you want.[5]

- *An ally will stay stable when things get difficult.* At crisis points it falls to you to signal to your child, loudly and clearly, that you can be depended upon. Things will sometimes get tough as you stand by your exceptional child who's rejecting gender conventions. They won't be tough all of the time, and they won't stay tough forever. What your child ideally needs, at times such as these, is to witness your steadiness. And, if not your steadiness, then your refusal to jump ship in any set of circumstances at all.

---

5   The parenting style you use with your child will have different consequences and is well documented. For an accessible guide to why authoritative parenting is a wise choice, see: Dewar, G. (2013) 'The authoritative parenting style: Warmth, rationality, and high standards.' *Parenting Science*. Available at www.parentingscience.com/authoritative-parenting-style.html, accessed on 27 July 2017.

The Four Keys an ally needs

Listening

Listening is the first thing we need to remember when we begin to communicate with someone, and it's normally the first thing we forget, too. Mark Nepo, the poet and teacher, believes that 'listening is the doorway to everything that matters'.[6] Listening isn't something we do so well in modern cultures; and doing so with our hearts, even less so. Yet all of us know how we feel when we've been deeply listened to: respected, more understood and more able to hear what the other person may have to say. Listening is a mysterious exchange. It's about opening up a space for another person, and emptying ourselves out, to hear missives from their inner world. It runs directly counter to our 'fix-it' mentality and the need to do things at speed. True listening is an act of receiving, which leads on to understanding, evaluating, remembering and responding. As a parent, caregiver and ally, listening is a superpower we can draw on anytime, anywhere and with anyone. Most importantly, it's a skill that can be developed. Listening is also a passport to peace of mind.

When my kids were very young, I made the decision that I wanted to be a listening parent, especially when it carried weight. I knew then that I'd have to grow broad shoulders, too. I wanted my kids to feel they could confide in me, so learning to listen, not react, became a chief priority of mine. Over the years, from toddlers to teenagers, I was seriously tested in my resolve. Sometimes it didn't hold up and oftentimes it did. I'm still practising. Many times my teenagers confided things that left me staring up at the ceiling a long time after they'd gone to bed. But I never regretted my decision to be a mother who listened – ever. The work it entailed proved insignificant compared to the consolation of knowing they could turn to me, whatever might be happening in their lives. As one

---

6   Nepo, M. (2013) *Seven Thousand Ways to Listen*. New York, NY: Atria Books.

grandmother expressed to me when she was reflecting back on her close relationship with her gender-questioning granddaughter:

> The most useful thing you can do ever, is to listen. Always be open and just listen. And so you have to be a receiver. As soon as you start putting out what someone should do, the person talking will close up. If you listen, they'll open up and start telling you stuff. The difference between listening and advice-giving, is the difference between asking and not telling. And trust them. Trust that they'll find their way and get it right for themselves.

Imagination

I wonder what your first thoughts are when you read the word 'imagination'. So often we think of it as existing primarily in the realm of childhood, or to do with a specific project, rather than an everyday attribute that we use in all weathers and many situations. Imagining is part of what we do, and how we function. It's a central faculty of being human. Think about it: we imagine what our vacation is going to be like, we imagine our perfect job, we imagine how it might feel to be sick or live in a specific location, we imagine a future with a person we've made a commitment to and we imagine transforming an empty house into a home. As new parents, we are often thrown into the arms of our imagination to help us make sense of our tiny baby's needs. The whole evolution of human beings, as a species, has depended on our capacity to first visualise, then materialise, possibilities. Without sufficient imaginative powers we're unable have faith. Faith is to do with trusting in something unseen, something we hold inside ourselves as a possibility or a truth. I'm paying a great deal of attention to writing this book at the moment. Consequently, words are getting down on the page and a manuscript is, slowly, materialising. Beneath this surface dynamic, my imaginative powers continue to create and stoke a vision of a world where gender diversity isn't a problem anymore, where children are given the freedom to express their felt sense of gender unreservedly. My imagination takes me to this place. I believe in the possibility of it. Can you imagine anything of this world too?

The capacity to imagine, then, is not something to be indulged in our spare time, or ignored as frivolous. It can be kept, half-asleep, in the realm of the everyday or it can be used with awareness and specific intent. It's a dynamic, energetic force with the power to create reality. That's why Albert Einstein, one of the most renowned scientists that has ever lived, told us, 'Imagination is more important than knowledge.' What a resource to have at our disposal.

As an ally, make the choice to use your imagination in ways that will serve you, your child and your family. Inhibit your imagination from fuelling your fears. Choose instead to harness its enormous power for good. Allow it to galvanise your attention and energy positively, and this will lead to associations and insights about your child you've never had before. Your imagination will enable you to relate to your child's emotional and psychological states in fresh ways, and become more alert to the effects of your own words and actions as you do so.

Empathy

Empathy is an outcome of imagination combined with the willingness to be fully 'present' to another person's experience. Empathy helps to mediate fear. It reduces the risk of excessively rational, wildly fluctuating or painfully irrational reactions, because it's relational. It's about understanding, not reacting. Empathy is essential to facilitating the gender journey unfolding in your home. I once heard this powerful emotion described as the 'capacity to step into someone else's world without leaving a footprint'. I think that's a beautiful description of what I'm talking about here. When we receive empathy, we feel seen and we feel acknowledged. Most of us don't need or want to be agreed with all of the time, and all of us want to feel heard and respected. Our children are no exception to this.

Empathy isn't sympathy. Sympathy is born out of our own perceptions about how something is for someone else. Sympathy is saying 'Yes, I agree, that's a really horrible thing to have to be going through.' Empathy is different; it's only ever about the other person's experience and not your own. It's about recognising and understanding someone else's lived reality, whether you 'agree' with it, or not. An empathic person offers their shoulder as a pillow to soothe, not as a rock that will numb. Put simply, a parent or caregiver who is empathic can suspend their own sense of self for a short time and imagine, with deep emotional resonance, how it must be to live inside their child's skin.

Courage

Courage means 'to be filled with heart'. It is the centrepiece of our work as allies. Heart has come to symbolise love in our culture, so when we love our children unconditionally, it means that we have an abundance of courage at our disposal. I believe love is a verb, an action word. Love, courage and action go together. Courage will provide the fuel to question beliefs you once depended upon or to initiate conversations with yourself you never imagined you could have. Courage will spark conversations with others that you once would have dampened down. It will enliven every decision you make with authenticity. Courage will push through your fear. It will embolden you to ask why things are as they are, to challenge the dominant version of the truth and demand what can be done to change the situation. You won't be satisfied with having our own rights protected if those you care about are denied the same privileges. Courage is a small wavering flame, a single flare across the sky, a blazing beacon, a fire, a volcano. Courage is saying 'yes' to life, to opening up to your situation and not allowing fear to dictate the conditions of this. Courage is your heart, full of love for your gender-expansive child, ready to act on their behalf.

The Four Keys – listening, imagination, empathy and courage – will unlock most, if not all, the barriers to accepting and protecting your gender-expansive child. Keep them to hand at all times. Now we're going to turn our faces towards 'All Things Gender', on our way to encountering the Gender Matrix, and what that means in the lives of all of us.

CHAPTER 2

ALL THINGS GENDER

None of us remember our first breath – the gasp that we meet the world with. Or the hands that first touch us. The eyes that search our body. The words that seal who we will be in the world. A girl or a boy.

The practice of gendering a child at birth is so commonplace we never even think about it. Yet our sex and our gender are different things. The term *sex* refers to genitals and sex organs, which are identified as female or male. An assumption is made at birth that a female infant will be a girl, or a male infant will be a boy; so gender is assumed and *assigned*. In some instances, the physiology of an infant doesn't easily fit into these typical sex categories, so they're categorised by the medical term 'intersex'.[1] Our *assigned* gender is what gets stamped onto our birth certificate, which is the most significant formal document we will ever own.

When a person's sense of gender identity matches their anatomical sex, they are known as *cisgender*. This is the reality, overwhelmingly, for most people. Consequently, this way of being is read as 'normal' and is assumed inevitable. In the adult world it looks like this: men

---

[1]   While people who are born intersex share similarities with people who are transgender – particularly a similar history of being shamed and discriminated against because of their conditions – the two experiences are different. Both, happily, are now being recognised and reclaimed as natural variations of human gender and anatomy. For further information, visit the website of the Intersex Society of North America at www.isna.org.

have penises and women have vaginas, and we expect our children to be made in our image. But in making sex and gender the same thing, we make wrong anyone who shows us that it isn't so.

As we begin to take this confusion apart and separate out two of the primary parts of identity, it can feel strange or even stressful. We're stretching our mind to go beyond the binary boxes it's been conditioned to tick as 'natural'. This threshold can also be an exciting one because, like all thresholds, there are fresh possibilities on the other side of it. So let's stretch a bit further and explore the three components that make up our gender identity: our *felt* sense of it, our gender expression and our sexual orientation.

Gender on the inside

Gender is how we feel on the inside of ourselves, which may or may not 'match' our body parts. It originates in our private, innermost feelings. Prior to Ruben's gender journey turning towards a horizon I'd never considered before, I'd rarely questioned my own identification as a woman. I only knew I was one, and it felt like a perfect fit for me. As I began to think in much greater depth about this, I also began to ask strangers and friends alike how they knew what their gender was. Everyone, without exception, began to give me a confident answer and then, as they considered it more, small frown lines appeared between their eyebrows and they began to stare at a spot in the distance. After further pauses and hesitation, the response was always the same: 'I know what my gender is – because I just do.' In other words, we know it because we feel it and not because we can objectively prove it. This perspective is, paradoxically, both radical and common sense too. Radical, because until recently, the received wisdom handed down from medics and mental health professionals is that gender aligns with genitals and is fixed by about three years of age. And, common sense, because when we pause and check whereabouts in our bodies our own gender identity sits, we realise it isn't between our legs after all.

The interplay of chromosomes, gonads and hormones in gender development is highly complex.[2] The debate about whether brains are hardwired to be male or female is on-going and loud. Perhaps Stephanie Brill and Rachel Pepper, the authors of *The Transgender Child,* frame these aspects in a way most of us can find useful:

> Some theories point to environmental influences, others to prenatal hormonal influence, but most agree that it (gender identity) is most likely determined before we are born. From this perspective the brain is a gendered organ and gender identity is not a conscious decision. People do not choose to feel like a boy or a girl, or like both, or neither. They simply are who they are. From this perspective, transgender people and all people whose gender identity does not align with their anatomical sex are simply born this way.[3]

Gender on the outside

The second component that supports a gendered sense of self is expression: our style of behaviour, clothing preferences, voice and body characteristics, as well as natural inclinations. When I began to consider this I was amazed at the variety of expression that existed across my friends and acquaintances, which I'd not registered before. I have a close male friend who is a sensitive introvert, small-boned and gentle in his communication style. Another who wears his long white hair loose, has tattoos all over his ample body and cries easily. One of my women friends shows 'unladylike' anger as keenly as affection and

---

2   Brill, S. and Pepper, R. (2008) *The Transgender Child.* San Francisco, CA: Cleis Press.
3   Brill, S. and Pepper, R. (2008) *The Transgender Child.* San Francisco, CA: Cleis Press, p.14.

wears clothes that range from feather boas to leather brogue shoes. In reality, gender expression is much more vivid and versatile than many of us realise. In the adult world it's also compounded by dress codes – formal or informal – that reinforce similarity. It's informative and amusing to acknowledge that children, when they're at work in play, will have none of the bland expression that we adults meekly conform to. Musing in this way is useful. It can point to and break down the assumptions we unconsciously carry about what makes a 'real' woman or man, or for that matter, girl or boy. None of us has escaped our own gender conditioning, and most of us unwittingly project at least some of it onto other people. It's important to remember, too, that gender expression can frequently be subject to outward influences that inhibit inward impulses. A person's ethnicity, class, culture or religion, for instance, may act as a brake on how free someone feels to express their gender openly. For some of those people, curbing their gender style may be the only way to guarantee some safety for themselves in the world.

Gender and sexual orientation

Gender and sexual orientation are frequently confused. Like siblings, they're closely related, yet separate and distinct from each other. Sexual orientation is about who we're attracted to and have romantic and/or sexual feelings for (or not, as is the case with asexual people). Our sexuality is how we choose to express our sexual orientation. Sexuality, collectively, is a landscape that shimmers with many textures, colours, shapes and shifting weather streams. And the diverse manifestation of it isn't a product of the modern world. A multitude of historical records and anthropological studies tell us otherwise.[4] Classical art and religion, Sufi poets and retrieved

---

4   Baird, V. (2001) *No-Nonsense Guide to Sexual Diversity.* Oxford: New Internationalist Publications.

histories abound with references to same-sex love and amorous ambitions.[5] But this isn't the story Western culture has told itself for the last several centuries is it? In this version, the landscape is colonised, cordoned off and heavily patrolled. There are boundary walls that mark out the territory of 'acceptable' consensual desire between adults. People who live outside of them, often can still be marked out as deviant in some way. The apparatus of this varies from place to place, but the motivation is always the same: to reinforce heterosexuality (commonly referred to as being 'straight') as the only legitimate expression of sexual desire.

Gender and sexuality are convoluted and conflated to such an extent in our culture that we use the word *sex* to refer to both our identity *and* our sexual conduct. They are different. As Andrew Solomon points out in his illuminating book, *Far from the Tree*, 'Trans children are not manifesting sexuality; they are manifesting gender. The issue is not whom they wish to be with, but who they wish to be.'[6] Many people feel discomfort and, sometimes, an indefinable disgust when a child cross-dresses outside of socially sanctioned situations. It took me time to identify, acknowledge and separate out the emotions Ruben's persistent cross-dressing provoked in me. These feelings were difficult to admit to and reflect on, even with the will to do so. When we use the words 'gender' and 'sex' interchangeably, and then add 'children' to that equation, it becomes taboo territory in the minds of almost all of us. Our mixed-up feelings stop us from thinking. We must speak about this confusion so we can unpack it. In doing so, we'll see the parts for what they are and begin to make sense of our responses and behaviour. If we don't untangle our feelings, they will not quietly go away. The risk is that our disturbed response may

5   Baird, V. (2001) *No-Nonsense Guide to Sexual Diversity*. Oxford: New Internationalist Publications.

6   Solomon, A. (2014) *Far from the Tree: Parents, Children and the Search for Identity*. London: Penguin Random House, p.598.

become a murky backwater of our consciousness. Then, without our awareness, it will seep into the lives of those we cherish the most.

Gender expression in children

Children don't arrive in the world with a 'one size fits all' label of either 'boy' or 'girl' attached to them. When it comes to gender, we seem to assume that they do. You and I both know this isn't the case. A newborn baby isn't yet tethered to the internal gender post that society will seek to cement into their psyche. For a brief time, the infant will be free. Left alone, children express their gender in diverse, fluid and contradictory ways. They do not naturally associate their genitals with a specific role they feel compelled to fulfil. This is something the adult world teaches them to do. Usually, by the time a child has seen five or six summers come and go, most little ones have learnt this lesson well.

I was present when Ruben was born. When his head crowned and my daughter prepared herself for the final push, I had a profound moment of knowing. I could only see a dark mass of hair, matted with fluid. Still as the eye of an owl. Ruben was between both worlds in that suspended second. The final contraction holding him back, then reaching its peak and expelling him from everything he had ever known. I have never forgotten that threshold moment and what it taught me. That with our first breath, the one we never remember, our pure state of being is lost. We are launched into a terrible reality we have no way of comprehending. And only parental devotion, love and sacrifice can mediate this experience.

A human baby is a marvellous creature. The learning curve they have to traverse from birth onwards is nothing short of awe-inspiring. Discovering how to suckle, crawl, use a spoon, fathom and acquire language, learning how to conceptualise, visualise, interact and become increasingly independent...this is creativity at its highest level. If a child has additional needs and has to 'double' adapt to their environment, then even more so. William Blake, the artist poet, who was a devotee of children, believed creativity was akin to following the 'Golden Thread'. We trust and celebrate – rightly so – the golden thread of growth and development our infants leverage their life energy around. When a child begins to dance as well as walk, or to sing as well as talk, we rejoice in their development. We do everything we can to support their emerging sense of who they are and what they're capable of. For many children, that same thread will compel them to live their gender identity in ways that are different to their peers. This is their authentic configuration. And it may require a considerable amount of time before its pattern is established.

We know that the vast majority of children who cross-dress and otherwise play at the edges of gender identity are, simply, not conforming to what's expected of them. Evidence now suggests that this is, in fact, more likely to be indicative of future sexual orientation, not their gender identity.[7] Very few of these children go on to become transgender.

Gender kaleidoscope

When children are permitted to follow the Golden Thread of their gendered selves, individuality will be their hallmark. Some may identify as transgender, others will be at home in their assigned sex yet ignore the prescribed gender norms, some may feel like a boy one day and a girl the next, or meld a number of gender aspects that feel 'right' to them. Any of these possibilities can be hard for us as parents and caregivers to grasp, let alone accept. It takes willingness, time and imagination to begin to familiarise your head and heart with them,

---

7   Ehrensaft, D. (2011) *Gender Born, Gender Made*. New York, NY: The Experiment LLC.

to recognise a horizon in your life that, until now, has been invisible. This shifting of perception is akin to seeing in the dark. First of all, everything we recognise is lost to our senses, and then patterns and shapes materialise in a new form. Eventually, we realise we actually do know where we are; what's different is that we're seeing it from a new perspective.

Gender Identity Research and Education Society (GIRES) estimates that 650,000 people in the United Kingdom experience some degree of gender nonconformity. This is an upward trend, with growth rates in children and young people seeking medical care increasing at 50 per cent per annum. Since the launch of GIRES's directory of local and national support groups in 2010, it has been accessed 2.3 million times.[8] In 2015/16, 969 children under the age of 18 were referred to the NHS dedicated Gender Identity Development Service (GIDS) in north London. Of these, 200 were 12 years or under. Only five years ago referrals amounted to 94 in total.[9] These figures, of course, preclude unknown numbers of children who are living their *felt*, not assigned, birth gender, and are uninvolved with clinical services. And there's a rapid growth of children and young people who refuse to identify with any categories despite, very often, enormous pressure to do so.

Dr Diane Ehrensaft, a developmental and clinical psychologist, and a leading advocate for gender-expansive children, makes the point that 'a spectrum is a very two-dimensional, linear concept, and doesn't give full weight to the myriad possibilities in establishing one's true gender identity'.[10] She more usefully constructs it as a web:

---

8   Visit www.gires.org.uk.
9   McKenzie, C. (2016) 'Child gender identity referrals show huge rise in six years.' BBC News, 11 February 2016. Available at www.bbc.co.uk/news/uk-england-nottinghamshire-35532491, accessed on 14 July 2017.
10   Ehrensaft, D. (2011) *Gender Born, Gender Made*. New York, NY: The Experiment LLC, p.4.

This web will take into account any particular child's assigned gender, that which appears on their birth certificate; the child's gender expressions – those feelings, behaviours, activities, and attitudes that communicate to both self and other, one's presentation of self as either male, female or other; and the child's core gender identity – the inner sense of self as male, female, or other.[11]

For over 35 years, the primary gender teachers of Dr Ehrensaft have been the children and young people with whom she's worked. This specialist faculty has taught her that while female, male and transgender identities exist, so too do many others. In her most recent book, *The Gender Creative Child*, she refers to these variations as the 'Gender Orchard' of apples, oranges and fruit salad. And in response to those people who insist gender should only conform to one of two boxes, she says this:

> From those gender creative people who experience it from this inside and those allies who know it from the outside comes an outcry: 'It's not a choice, it is who we are – male, female, or other. It just is.' Informed by all the children who have taught me what I know, I would say there is no better answer than that: it just is. Yet to say that it is not a choice does not mean that it is completely constitutional, determined by nature. It simply means that before we were born and then along our journey through life, a confluence of influences met, some flowing from nature, some from nurture, and some from the culture surrounding both nature and nurture.[12]

---

11   Ehrensaft, D. (2011) *Gender Born, Gender Made*. New York, NY: The Experiment LLC, p.4.
12   Ehrensaft, D. (2016) *The Gender Creative Child*. New York, NY: The Experiment, LLC, p.33.

Dr Ehrensaft appreciates that living with this sort of ambiguity, when a parent or caregiver may desperately need certainty, is enormously demanding. Surviving on the frontier, the place that's between certainty and the unknown, is a master class in stress management for many of us. The drive to find answers, or create a measure of security to counter gripping uncertainty, can propel us into quick decisions to alleviate our anxiety. These decisions might range from hurriedly seeking out a diagnosis and celebrating it as the new norm, to demanding that your child simply does as they're told. It might mean taking your child to a psychologist without any prior discussion or inviting your friends over for a 'coming out' party, without your child's consent. Relationships can become strained, parents can differ in their approach as to how to manage their child's welfare, and conflict can erupt. One way or another, we have to learn to steady ourselves at times like this; to step back, to take a breath; to ask ourselves out loud what we need, and then to motivate ourselves to find these resources. We may need confidential support, specific information, a hug, a mentor, time out, or time with our child without gender being the focus at all. Whatever it is, we must commit to resourcing ourselves because our child is counting on us. And because, above all else, we want to ensure that love remains the north star of all our decision-making.

So let's bring our attention fully to the cultural context we find ourselves in, to how the Gender Matrix works in practice. Let's look at why, and how, we're invested in teaching gender conformity to our children in the first place. There are valid reasons. We'll pause in this part of the territory, analysing and reflecting on them, before moving on. Then we'll scope out, and get ready to scale the defences of the Gender Matrix. From this vantage point, we'll learn to see with new eyes.

CHAPTER 3

ENCOUNTERING THE MATRIX

Encountering the Matrix in myself

Young children will engage with, explore and express their shifting realities with consummate ease, which is often why adults find their company so delightful. When Ruben first began to express a preference for girls' things, this was the only context we put his behaviour in. Before long, he had accrued a pink lunch box, three or four princess dolls, a bag full of sparkly jewellery and a flowery crockery set he served tea in to his soft toys. No-one in my immediate family was uncomfortable with these initial developments. For myself, I began to think that my grandson, like his uncle before him, might well be expressing behaviour that indicated a future sexual orientation. At this point in our story, I never imagined that Ruben's preferences said anything about his gender at all. To me, he was a 'girly-boy' and would most likely grow up to be the same sort of confident, loving and competent man my son is.

But reflecting back now, I see that I was uneasy with one thing in particular: Ruben's gender expression in public. The first time I tried to persuade Ruben out of one outfit and into another, he was about three-and-a-half and had started to assert a strong desire to wear girls' clothes. My daughter, son-in-law or myself didn't know quite what to make of this. I remember arriving at his house one afternoon to take him out for a 'treat'. When I entered the front room, he was leaping around on the settee and gleefully chanting, 'Nan-nee, Nan-nee'. He'd dressed himself for the occasion in his sister's pink and purple striped woollen tights and a white tee-shirt with a silver, glittery unicorn on it. My daughter, Jude, raised her eyebrows at me. Recalling it now, our conversation went something like this:

'Sweetheart, you're going to get cold in those tights.'

'But I want to wear them, Nanny.'

'I know, but you'll get cold and Nanny doesn't want you to.'

'They're really warm.'

'Let's put something else on.'

'I like the colours.'

'I know you do, darling. But trousers are better to go out in, don't you think?'

'These are nice tights.'

'Let me go and see what else you've got in your wardrobe, eh?'

I went into his bedroom and returned with some toddler's chinos in my hands. Ruben looked at them, looked at me, and then looked away. He sighed: 'Nanny, I don't feel like going out now.'

Up until this point, I'd imagined I was getting away with my softly spoken subterfuge. That Ruben, somehow, was fooled by my disingenuous remarks. But when I witnessed his bouncing three-year-old energy sink back into his muted words, I understood my actions weren't benign. Remorse is a powerful motivator for change. I knew then that my conduct had breached the bond of trust between my grandchild and myself. I could have tried to convince myself that my behaviour was 'understandable' and I was only protecting my grandson, but that would have been another lie. Remorse is also the precursor to repair. The issue wasn't Ruben's clothing; the issue was why I worried about it so much in the first place. The fact that Ruben couldn't outwardly articulate this for himself was irrelevant.

It's possible to carry an allegiance to something or someone and not be aware of it. I knew I had pledged myself to Ruben from the moment of birth, yet I had no idea about the pledge I'd unconsciously taken to the Matrix. I mistakenly thought I'd eradicated most of its sticky fingerprints on my psyche. But my allegiance had persisted and, what's more, the roots had put out tubers. Admitting to myself that I held some unconscious allegiance to the dominant Gender Matrix was not easy. Yet my behaviour showed me otherwise. Yes, at a deep just-out-of-my-awareness level I wanted to protect my grandson. At a gut, instinctive level I was sensing a threat that I hadn't even begun to articulate in any detail to myself. But, my resistance to enabling Ruben to expand his gender expression belied another truth too. In the small exchange I describe above, I'd modelled dishonesty, cowardice and a strong disregard for someone else's feelings. I'd compromised myself and my relationship with Ruben for fear of embarrassment and disapproval. From whom and about what? These were the questions I had to sit with until I got some answers that satisfied my conscience.

As the months passed, Ruben's preferences and requests became more insistent. I remember Jude calling me one day after she'd been out shopping for shoes for him. Ruben was pining for some shiny pink sandals. Faced with her son's innocent desire, and surrounded by boys' trainers standing sentry on grey and beige boxes, Jude hadn't known what to do. Later that day, the light in her child's eyes matched his glossy footwear as he ran to meet me when I arrived at his home. 'Nanny,' he declared, 'aren't they beautiful?'

Several months later, I found myself in a similar everyday shopping situation that ended differently. Ruben needed some nightclothes and I'd gone to buy some for him at my local shopping centre. After going in and out of several shops, I recall wandering around the final store with two children's dressing gowns, uniform in size, hanging over my arm. Yes, one was blue and one was pink. To anyone watching, I was a woman at ease, contemplating further purchases and taking her time. But in reality I was in conflict. Not only was I undecided about which item to buy, I was ferociously criticising myself for deliberating about it in the first place. How did my values and my indecision add up? Why was I cowing before standards I deplored? And why on earth was I allowing myself to be held hostage by a colour? Round and round my thoughts went as I rotated the aisles, trying to separate out my feelings like a pack of dogs baying for a fight. In the end, exhausted, I put both dressing gowns back and chose some boys' pyjamas that could just about pass as unisex. I left the store feeling miserable and defeated.

Ruben's parents took each step with their child deliberately, thoughtfully and empathically. As his primary carers, they understood the power was all theirs to control his gender expression. They began to educate themselves about gender identity. Everyone who loved Ruben unconditionally became part of the conversation. It wasn't always easy. Gradually they began to facilitate more and more opportunities for him to express his felt gender authentically in the world. And there could be no denying how outrageously happy this made our bright and communicative child. On this basis, my support was absolute. And, I remained conflicted in a way that made no sense to me at all, so I knew I had inner work to do before I could understand why.

Looking back, I feel compassion for myself now. Things were moving quickly in my family and I wasn't processing them at the same speed. I was talking to close friends about what was happening but I was careful not to discuss my personal anxieties with Ruben's parents and I didn't know anyone who had had a similar experience. Consequently, those anxieties created states of emotional freefall in me where, sometimes, I couldn't quite grasp hold of anything solid. I also had a belief operating that *I should feel okay* about what was happening. This, perhaps more than anything else, prevented me from accepting my vulnerability. It was many months before I began to loosen this knot and make sense of what was going on inside of me.

Encountering the Matrix around us

It never occurred to me that gender would be the territory where my next level of development lay because, for most of my life, I've had it within my sights. I vividly recall being as young as six and watching the television when the English band The Honeycombs appeared on it. Wide-eyed and delighted, I was transfixed by their female drummer. Of course I didn't know then what I know now: women weren't supposed to do this. Honey Lantree was in the vanguard of female pop musicians in the 1960s. Her behaviour felt transgressive to me and it was her audacity, not her talent, that captured my imagination so fully. As I watched her play, I was peeking outside the confines of my gender education and yearning for a freedom I didn't feel entitled to. I've pursued this freedom over a lifetime, shaped by my own personal history, choices and circumstances. I believed I'd successfully re-landscaped the Matrix in my psyche. But my resistance to Ruben's gender-expansive behaviour taught me differently. I'd only dug into, turned over and re-planted the aspects of gender that mattered to me. This included how boys and men, as well as girls and women, are powerfully groomed to fit into their respective roles. My frame of reference, unknowingly, was bound by the binary. The gender book I was consulting didn't include whole sections of the human family. Ruben added these pages for me.

I began to explore all the contradictions I felt in depth; through journalling, reading and conscious conversations with people I trusted. Gradually, the pieces began to fall into place. And one stood out above all the others. My gender politics had always pivoted on the relationship between men, women and the patriarchal system we live under. Over the years, I'd recognised how toxic patriarchy is for all parties, while continuing to bear witness to women's experience specifically. I'd opposed sexism and homophobia wherever I came across it, including within myself. I'd examined my own unearned privilege as a heterosexual person, and worked on creating a healthy sense of entitlement for myself as a woman, and as someone from a working-class background. And...in all of this, I had failed to recognise the range of human experience outside of the binary construct. If, as William Shakespeare declares, 'all the world's a stage, and men and women merely players', then my view had been obscured by two pillars. Consequently, in my psyche, a place had not been prepared to receive Ruben's reality, in all its fullness, as it flowed towards my own. Perhaps this isn't surprising in some ways. Often we only begin to think about something deeply when it touches our own life. But there's a far more perilous and pervasive reason my consciousness hadn't expanded.

Consensus reality

Consensus reality is the idea that 'reality' comes about through social agreement, not because it has anything to do with a definitive and absolute truth. My searching and studying began to suggest that the prevailing consensus reality had seduced me into believing gender was only two dimensional. Because this particular consensus reality has held sway for so long and with such force, Western society has come to mirror it as 'truth'. But as I stood back far enough from my own experience, I came to recognise that it depended on one thing and one thing alone: compliance. Consensus reality isn't about truth; it's about perception. So it stands to reason that when we change our perception, we change our reality. How we *look* determines what we actually see.

Gender diversity not only occurs across the globe, but in some parts of the world a formal role exists between the male/female binary that essentially constitutes a third gender. Whether this is the *muxe* in Mexico, the *hijra* in South East Asia or the *mahu* in Hawaii, these communities testify to life outside of the binary. A positive social context will, inevitably, shape the gaze of everyone else around these people and, as such, determine what they 'see'. We also know, beyond doubt, that transgender people have existed in most cultures across time.[1] Their history is not a public one. The retrieval of *any* history that has been eclipsed is important for all of us. It reveals that bias, deceit, politics and power have more to do with recorded events than facts, figures and men charging into battle on flag-clad horses. It reminds us that only the 'winners' get to roll out their version of the truth, however partial or partisan it is. A retrieved history teaches us that 'reality' can be questioned and culture isn't written in stone. When we spend time educating ourselves about missing pieces, we learn to fill in the blanks. We begin to understand the story beneath the fabrication. Over the field of time, many retrieved histories have begun to emerge: the histories of women, immigrants, slaves, sexual minorities and people living with impairments, to name a few. The attempt to erase them was calculated.

When something or someone doesn't get recognised, their story and all that this represents has no part in constructing the rolling unfolding of consensus reality. When the footprints of a community are swept away, or cemented over, the intent is to leave no visible trail for others to follow. In effect, the dominant group creates a pretence, culture is impoverished, amnesia is rewarded and gross inequalities persist.

European explorers and colonialists set out to decimate 'heathen' indigenous cultures.[2] Driven by religious and political affiliations, they justified ruthless violence and unrelenting oppression. Destroying evidence of 'gender deviance' was integral to this mission.[3] Through the work of writers and activists such as Will Roscoe, Randy

1   Baird, V. (2001) *No-Nonsense Guide to Sexual Diversity.* Oxford: New Internationalist Publications. Ehrensaft, D. (2011) *Gender Born, Gender Made.* New York, NY: The Experiment, LLC.Garbacik, J. (2013) *Gender and Sexuality for Beginners.* Danbury, CT: For Beginners, LLC.
2   Alaers, J. (2010) 'Two-spirited people and social work practice: Exploring the history of Aboriginal gender and sexual diversity.' *Critical Social Work 11* (1).
3   Alaers, J. (2010) 'Two-spirited people and social work practice: Exploring the history of Aboriginal gender and sexual diversity.' *Critical Social Work 11* (1).

Connor and Leslie Feinberg among others, the respectable tradition of gender diversity in Indigenous communities is being reclaimed. This catalogue of work demonstrates that alternative gender roles and identities were accepted, and often honoured, in many cultures. Shamanic traditions across all continents, before there was contact with Europe, often embraced this diversity as testimony to spiritual powers. A transgender identity was understood to be a 'threshold' state, which meant such a person could move between worlds and communicate with spirits. So these individuals frequently served their communities as guides, guardians, ceremonial leaders and shape-shifters.[4] Meanwhile, others, who identified similarly, occupied more commonplace roles as anyone else might do. What's clear is that gender difference was welcomed as an asset to these groups, rather than as an assault on their way of perceiving the world.

First Nations groups in North America comprehended reality as a sacred web of life in which everyone had their own unique place. Intuiting a child's life quest to discover their unique role was a holy responsibility within the community. If a child's behaviour suggested a transgender orientation, rituals existed in some communities to verify this. In one such ritual, 'the bow or the basket', a paper or grass circular structure would be constructed, with these two items inside. The bow represented male gender and the basket, female. The child would be instructed to go inside the structure and wait for a signal. When the signal came, they knew they had to grab one of the items and run. Then the elders set fire to the frame. If the child, under such intense survival pressure, chose an item typically associated with their opposite sex, this was conclusive evidence of their status and it determined how they would be socialised thereafter.[5] In this circumstance, what concerned the elders was authenticating the

---

4   Wood, B. N. (2012) 'The Shaman transformed.' *Sacred Hoop Magazine* 77, 18–21. Connor, R. P. L. (2000) 'Men, women, gate-keepers, and fairy mounds.' *Parabola* 25(1), 71–5.

5   Alaers, J. (2010) 'Two-spirited people and social work practice: Exploring the history of Aboriginal gender and sexual diversity.' *Critical Social Work 11* (1).

child's inclination, not influencing it. These divining rituals were vital. They conferred on an individual an identity, respect and a purpose. The prevailing consensus reality, where gender diversity was seen as a natural variation of life, was inclusive. And, in being so, a home already existed in the minds and hearts of community members to welcome these children into.

The frontier of change

Despite radical cultural transformation since the 1960s, gender remains the social centre of gravity across the globe. Why this is so remains a hotly contested issue. All these viewpoints have their own vehement supporters and vocal detractors, and there is barely, if any, neutral territory between them. What cannot be refuted, though, is that within our lifetimes, ideals of identity, romance and sex have altered dramatically and, in turn, have dramatically altered people's perceptions in Western culture. This hasn't occurred in a vacuum. The urgent sustained work of political activists and their allies, over decades, galvanised the social change we now see in the West, despite concerted attempts to hide, destroy or overlook it.[6] But just as a sand bar constantly changes its shape and location as the river rises and falls, so too have these groups survived and overcome the currents of conservatism compelling them to disperse. Their mettle, sacrifice and zeal have shaped the coast of human geography beyond all recognition in the last 60 years.

People who express their sexuality and gender in non-typical ways enjoy more freedom than ever before in the modern world. It might seem as though their full human rights are secured because of this. Not so. In 77 countries homosexuality is still a crime, with

---

6   Garbacik, J. (2013) *Gender and Sexuality for Beginners*. Danbury, CT: For Beginners, LLC.

India reinstating a 153-year-old colonial-era law criminalising gay sex in 2013. The belief that the tide of vitriolic anti-LGBTQ (lesbian, gay, bisexual, transgender and questioning and/or queer) legislation engulfing African countries is tantamount to 'gay genocide' is increasing. In response, Ugandan activists recently launched and distributed 15,000 copies of a new magazine, *Bombastic*, designed to reclaim their own stories and reach out to their enemies. Given that the forefather of their movement, David Kato, was murdered in 2011 after his name was published in a magazine calling for the execution of gay people, this is an astounding act of bravery. We must be mindful when we're thinking about gender and sexual diversity to branch outwards from a position of cultural humility. It might be easy to assume that opposition to both is predominantly located in countries far away from the shores we call home. That would be a mistake. The extreme American Christian Right, for instance, is understood by many to be the raging fuel beneath the attacks on gender justice and LGBTQ rights in Africa.[7] In Europe and the United States, patients often find themselves humiliated and harassed by a medical system that is supposed to be serving them.[8] Self-harm, unsurprisingly, is a desperate response to the intolerance,

7   Baptise, N. and Foreign Policy in Focus (2014) 'It's not just Uganda: Behind the Christian right's onslaught in Africa.' *The Nation*. Available at www.thenation.com/article/its-not-just-uganda-behind-christian-rights-onslaught-africa, accessed on 14 July 2017.
Sesange, E. (2014) 'Is Africa on the road to a gay genocide?' *The Gay Star News*, 4 September, 2014.
8   Amnesty International (2014) *The State Decides Who I Am: Lack of Recognition for Transgender People*. Available at www.es.amnesty.org/uploads/media/The_state_decide_who_I_am._Febrero_2014.pdf, accessed on 15 July 2017.
Solomon, A. (2014) *Far from the Tree: Parents, Children and the Search for Identity*. London: Penguin Random House.
GATE Civil Society Expert Working Group (2013) *Critique and Alternative Proposal to the 'Gender Incongruence in Childhood' Category in ICD-11*, Buenos Aires, 4–6 April, 2013. Available at https://globaltransaction.files.wordpress.com/2012/03/critique-and-alternative-proposal-to-the-_gender-incongruence-of-childhood_-category-in-icd-11.pdf, accessed on 14 July 2017.

discrimination and violence these individuals sometimes suffer.[9] Marco Perolini, Amnesty International's expert on discrimination, commented on a report about the experience of transgender people in Europe that they were subject to 'blatant state discrimination'.[10] Diversity, as we know, is a fact. Inclusion, we must never forget, is a choice.

Thankfully, there's reason to feel tremendous hope, irrespective of the immense challenges that still exist. South Africa's Nobel Peace Prize laureate, retired Archbishop Desmond Tutu, remains a powerful advocate for sexual minority rights in Africa. Pope Francis has publicly declared, 'Who am I to judge gay people?', and has had personal meetings with a number of LGBTQ activists and individuals. His leadership is signalling an attitude of compassionate inclusiveness which, even a decade ago, seemed impossible to imagine. Twenty-seven countries have legalised same-sex marriage around the world, including most recently the United States, the Republic of Ireland, Greenland and Colombia. In April 2015, Malta adopted a Bill, the Gender Identity, Gender Expression and Sex Characteristics Act, which recognises the right of each person to their gender identity and its free development. This trailblazing legislation is underpinned by a comprehensive education policy. The European Court of Human Rights ruled in April 2017 that requiring transgender people to undergo sterilisation, in order to have their gender recognised, violates their human rights. Sweden has become the first country in the world to pay compensation to Swedish transgender people in recognition of the crime committed by the state.

As the 21st century begins to imprint itself on history, it's indisputable that we're at a tipping point in relation to gender

---

9   See previous footnote.

10   Amnesty International (2014) *Europe: Transgender people face discrimination and inhuman treatment.* Available at www.amnesty.org/en/latest/news/2014/02/europe-transgender-people-face-discrimination-and-inhuman-and-degrading-treatment, accessed on 15 July 2017.

identity. More and more children and young people are traversing gender territory that has been taboo in the mainstream imagination until now. And, for an increasing number, the adults around them are prepared to be the foot soldiers on the frontier of this change. Such allegiance constitutes radical social activism. When a young child disavows their assigned birth gender, this not only scrambles the social order we've all internalised as 'natural', but it also undermines the very system that has written the rules. Parents and caregivers do not step lightly into this domain. The gender-expansive child meets a world that is hardly prepared for the encounter. But consensus reality is being redefined as gender diversity zigzags across the globe in dynamic ley lines. For some, these shifts are revolutionary; and for others, repugnant. Between both these two poles every other view jostles for position. Many people are bewildered by such momentous legal and social revisions within a generation, and this may be true for you. That's understandable – because, while I've cast a sweeping look at how sexual and gender diversity is prospering or not across the globe, right here and now in your home there's a child shuffling the gender cards and you don't know which way they're going to stack up.

CHAPTER 4

INVESTING IN THE MATRIX

We all know, on a deep primal level that 'fitting in' to both our family and culture is a survival imperative. From cradle to grave we are bound by this affiliation. So when a six-year-old boy adorns his hair with orange daisies, or a seven-year-old girl insists she wants her hair shorn off, they're stepping into risky territory. What should we do with children who do not fit into neat, tidy boxes? Should we squeeze them into these confined spaces? Press the crowns of their heads towards their knees and burden their shoulders with the weight of consensus reality? These little ones are simply expressing a preference, not trying to upset anyone. They don't know that, eventually, the wrath of the Matrix might fall across their bare backs. It's we, their parents and caregivers, who hold this knowledge; who, somehow, know where 'the line is' and what could happen if it gets crossed. And this, more often than not, creates a fierce undertow of fear in our minds and hearts. It's no surprise that we teach our children to conform.

There are two primary processes that ensure, to a greater or lesser extent, that they do. You and I have a deep knowledge of both, because each of them has intimately shaped who we are. The first is what developmental psychologists call 'attachment'; this is the impulse to form deep and enduring emotional bonds to others, which exist over time and space. And the second is 'acculturation', which is the manner by which an infant acquires the culture of the society they've been born into. Both processes, consciously or not, govern most parents and caregivers to either explicitly, or tacitly, promote the Gender Matrix.

Attachment

Children must achieve two things to ensure their survival in the world. The first is to be claimed by a family community as one of their own, and the second is to sufficiently attach to a caregiver who will meet their needs and protect them. In other words they must, by all means possible, find a way to *belong*. Without belonging, a human baby is destined to perish.[1] In most circumstances, a fully claimed child is a safe child. When parents, grandparents and other significant adults meet the infant, the experience is often akin to falling in love. Very often, no other baby is as beautiful, as curious or as delightful. The alchemy of the bonding process is at work in these positive life-affirming illusions. After a newborn has been claimed, then the primary carers must learn to *attune* to their child, to participate in a devout dance, predicting and responding to the needs of their infant, which will pattern the baby's brain in highly sophisticated and complex ways. Following this, the infant will learn to reciprocate and understand that their carer has needs and feelings too, and so the circle of connectedness is established. A sense of self begins, first and foremost then, through *identification* with others. From this position of strength, a toddler will begin to separate out from their caregiver and make the astonishing discovery that they are a person in their own right and can act independently. This is known as *differentiation*. And it's a developmental phase that children revisit again, usually with some gusto, during adolescence.

---

1   Cairns, K. and Fursland, E. (2008) *Building Identity: A Training Programme.* London: British Association for Fostering and Adoption.

As adults, we continue to participate in this complex choreography of who and what we identify with, and who and what we separate from, throughout our lives. This is the bread and butter of sameness and difference, which we negotiate on a daily basis. Many factors govern our aptitude with this, not least the rules, regulations and expectations we internalised, as children, from our own parents, relatives and communities. Our sense of morality, values and principles will have been hewn out of such council as we found our feet in the world. Many of these directives will have been useful, important and ultimately enriching to us. And some of them will not have been. It's sobering to realise we can still cling to certain rules, even when we know they're harmful to us now. Instead, we find ourselves behaving like 'adapted' children who can only be compliant, rather than adults who know the value of healthy independence and exercise it openly. Inevitably, many of the inhibitions we've inherited will be to do with gender. Our task, as allies, is to sift through them. We must look for bias, scrutinise what we believe, listen to our own opinions and observe our attitudes about gender. Then we must decide for ourselves which of them bring health to the family we've created or the family we're now part of.

According to attachment theory, when a child is securely attached to their carer they will have internalised a template that the world is safe and their needs will be met.[2] The attachment process is an astounding feat of nature. It ensures survival, even if familial bonds are only just adequate. When attachments are strong and robust, a child will almost always thrive. This is the paradox at the heart of attachment. When we claim and commit to a child, our subsequent investment in their survival barely falls short of overwhelming. We may find ourselves, repeatedly, in a social double bind: allow the child to be 'who they are' and risk them being misunderstood, or teach

---

2   Cairns, K. and Fursland, E. (2008) *Building Identity: A Training Programme*. London: British Association for Fostering and Adoption.

them to conform and risk sacrificing their individuality. Parents understand that membership in our modern-day tribes will afford our children a degree of safety in an unpredictable world. But we also know that this comes at a cost. And the cost, to a great extent, is blending in over standing out. In the end, conforming leads to approval, and approval leads to inclusion. This is why we teach our kids to keep in step – it's the good intention beneath our insistence.

Zoe is mum to Nickie, who, from a very young age, was a 'tomboy'. This wasn't any sort of problem for Zoe, a creative woman who is accepting of difference, colourful in both appearance and words, and clearly generous-hearted. It also didn't present any risk to her: 'It's acceptable isn't it? No-one bats an eyelid. There wasn't anything to think about.' But, as Nickie's gender-questioning behaviours increasingly dodged gender norms, Zoe's anxieties grew about her daughter fitting in at school:

> I said to her, 'Now you're going to big school, and you're starting to get some boobs, you need to start wearing a bra. Y'know, it can be a little sports bra.' I knew it was going to be an issue. I explained to her, 'I understand, I get you don't want to, but you'll be the only girl with your boobs out. Do you really want that?' Y'know, I felt mean putting it on the line. But that's what was going to happen. I kind of made her. I said, 'You're just going to bloody have to…' In the end, with the bra thing, it was an issue. A sticking point for the first year of big school. I stopped hassling her because I could see it was doing her head in, in a different kind of way. I could see it was really paining her inside. I thought, 'Oh fuck it, I'm not gonna make my child feel bloody depressed about wearing a bra. It's stupid. If she can figure out a way of just getting changed, I'll leave it to her.'

Zoe was able to differentiate between her needs and her child's, even though, initially, the two felt incompatible. She stayed open and tuned it to what was happening for her child. Consequently, Zoe found a middle ground when she took an informed, not foolish, risk in trusting her daughter's capacity to cope.

When we teach our children to conform, it provides us with an illusion of control because, ultimately, we know we can never fully protect any of them, no matter what we do. While this is understandable, it's also flawed thinking. And flawed thinking can lead to flawed caregiving if we're not prepared to reflect on it, as Zoe did. There are alternatives, as Jude, my daughter, has taught me:

> Yes, I feel like I've had to introduce Ruby to some of the realities of life that I wouldn't normally have talked about to her about at such a young age. But at the same time I thought, 'What I'm going to do is allow my child to be who she is, because that's who she's repeatedly saying she is.' I said to everyone from the beginning, and it gave me strength, 'I'm going to bring up a child who knows how to defend herself, who can stand up for her own rights, who understands she has rights. I'm going to resource her and do everything I can to enable her to be the person that she is, and to be happy as the person that she is.'

Parents who persist in cajoling and pressurising their gender-expansive child to change may justify their actions as love. Honest self-reflection may show them differently. It's likely, if not definite, that a need for approval, reassurance or security is motivating them to do so. This is slippery territory. In the end, the child may feel that their belonging in the family is conditional on their obedience and not related to their worth at all.

Culture and how we learn to fit in

Culture is a far-reaching and complex concept, and one that touches every person on the planet. Put simply, 'culture' refers to a group or community with which we share common experiences that tailor the way we understand the world. Some groups we're born into, such as gender, 'race' or national origin; other groups we join or become part of, such as married, disabled, professional or student. Because we all belong to many different groups, we belong to many cultures at once, though we often forget this. That's what happens when we become acculturated. We internalise the norms, rules and expectations of our group and rarely think about them. Like driving, our feet move on the pedals and our hands move at the wheel with no conscious awareness until, that is, something unexpected happens.

Human beings are highly social creatures and we band together instinctively. We're also sophisticated creatures. This combination of being social and sophisticated means that we don't have one fixed identity or sense of self.[3] Instead we have different identities at different times with fluctuating value, depending on the groups we're part of. Social identity theorists might break it down like this: a woman, who is a senior executive in her company, has a great deal of status in work; at home she feels entirely impotent as the daughter of a mother with Alzheimer's disease; and with her peers she feels on guard and diminished as the sister of a brother who is in prison for fraud. As this example shows, some aspects of our identity are given, some are chosen and others arise out of adversity and accident, which we have little control over.

The groups we're part of have a significant bearing on our identity and whether we feel good about ourselves or not. Our self-esteem is

3   Rudman, L. A. and Glick, P. (2008) *The Social Psychology of Gender: How Power and Intimacy Shape Gender Relations.* New York, NY: The Guilford Press. McLeod, S. (2007) *Social Psychology.* Available at www.simplypsychology.org/social-identity-theory.html, accessed on 22 July 2017.

enhanced when the groups we belong to have some sort of prestige. We feel as though we matter more, purely by association. In order to maximise our positive self-image we'll often emphasise the status of 'our' group, both implicitly and explicitly, and through a variety of means. Dress code generally, and uniforms particularly, demonstrate this point well. From military personnel through to inner-city gang members, haute-couture designers and high-court judges, dress codes share one thing in common: they are making a statement about relative power and they do so through showcasing status.

To consolidate a perceived advantage, people actively compare their group with others and this is when 'in-group/out-group' behaviours start to proliferate. You'll be familiar with these behaviours even if you've never referred to them in this way before. Sometimes they're 'jokey' and often sarcastic, and the underlying message is clear: your place here is conditional. Other times a comment or behaviour is so razored, there's no mistaking its purpose. In group/out group behaviours might include competitive actions designed to discredit opponents, withholding resources to undermine them or spreading rumours that correspond with negative stereotypes about them. These actions might be directed at a specific group, or specifically at someone who is new to a group, or needs to be part of it for a certain period of time. The common intent of all such behaviours is to alienate and exclude people, particularly those who are judged to be 'outsiders'.[4]

There was a time in my professional life when I was targeted in this way with some force. I was employed in a consultancy role, within a hierarchical organisation that was predominantly male. The identity of most employees was profoundly invested in maintaining the traditional roots of the organisation and they struggled with

---

4   Clements, P. and Spinks, T. (2009) *The Equal Opportunities Handbook: How to Recognise Diversity, Encourage Fairness and Promote Anti-Discriminatory Practice.* London: Kogan Page, 2009. Mindell, A. (1995) *Sitting in the Fire.* Portland, Oregon: Lao Tse Press.

cultural change. I was frequently with different close-knit teams who socialised, as well as worked, together. My footing as an outsider was precarious and this message was reinforced at almost every turn. When I walked into a room, I was stepping into the territory of the 'in-group', and everything about me represented 'out-group'. I was a woman, I was not a member of the organisation, and my remit was to question the status quo. The behaviours I met with ranged from ignoring me when I arrived, sitting in silence when I asked a question, commenting on my clothes, withholding practical information, using technical terms and phrases I didn't understand and aggressively questioning my mandate for working within the organisation. Occasionally I would be happily surprised and, you can imagine, not a little relieved when a group responded differently and opened up a temporary space for me. Then we could work collaboratively together for the benefit of all.

Usually a person reacts with one of three options if they're being 'refused entry' into a group they want or need to be part of: they erase all their individuality and assimilate into the group's culture, they challenge and confront the group, or they shrink to effectively become invisible in it. None of these responses are sustainable in the long term because all of them become exhausting. Many, if not all of us, will have personal experience of being part of an 'out-group', if only temporarily. We rarely forget it; from playgrounds and sports teams, through to factory floors, staff rooms and social clubs, 'entry' is conditional. We discover this, to our detriment, when we find the way barred to us.

There is an antidote to exclusion that goes some way to minimising the harmful effects of being targeted because you carry a difference. And that antidote is community, which we'll be looking at later on in the book. For now, we'll keep in mind the three distinct stages of group membership. First, we *categorise* ourselves as similar to others, then we adopt the *identity* of the groups we've categorised ourselves as being part of, then we tend to *compare* the groups we belong to with others. Obviously, if our self-esteem is to be maintained, it's essential that our group compares favourably to others. Material, emotional and psychological resources are all at stake here. Group life is a serious business.

So, what's all this got to do with your child and your circumstances?

If you think about it, a child's gender story always begins *before* birth in the imagination of parents and even extended family members. Conception is the opening line. A pregnant woman will be asked by both friends and strangers, 'Would you like a boy or a girl?' Or, more immediate still, 'Do you know what you're having?' In the minds of most people all over the world what precedes this question is the desire to categorise. The mystery of the child's sex strongly influences pre-birth behaviour. Friends will frequently hold off buying gifts until the baby is born, and relatives will be hoping the couple 'get' what they want. Pillow talk often includes how the unborn child will companion either parent in the blue or pink future of their imagination, and if the sex is established beforehand, specific actions like decorating a nursery often parallel gender norms. Many a large family exists because one or both parents wanted to realise their wish for the opposite-sex child to the ones they already have, and in some cultures one sex is highly prized over the other. Gender assignment is a forceful example of group membership and it counts whether we want it to or not.

Let me give you an example from my own life as a young woman who had just given birth to her second child. When my daughter was returned to my bedside in a cot shortly after her delivery, I was dismayed that the blanket covering her was blue. I asked the nurse to please change it. I wanted the world to celebrate I'd had a girl; how would the world know if the colour she was hidden beneath wasn't pink? I knew, rationally, my request amounted to waving a patriotic gender flag. But my politics were subsumed in a passionate desire to announce my baby's gender identity and I chose the most conventional of ways to do so, the underlying motivation being to signal which group my child belonged in: mine. It can be argued, of course, that my actions made no discernible difference to my daughter. But the point is they made a difference to me and I was her primary caregiver.

Boys this side, girls that side...

Newborn infants, before they've even been put to their mother's breast, are placed first in their assigned gender group. Thereafter, the caregivers around them begin to socially induct them into their respective gender roles. Even parents who are determined not to do this fall foul of their own internalised conditioning, as I did.[5] If we cast our gaze towards that rare minority of parents who dare to do otherwise; who dare to refrain from disclosing the sex of their child, what do we see? They invariably face controversy, disapproval and sometimes hostility. Such parents are regarded either as radical or stupid, and treated accordingly. In short, their transgression is tantamount to gender blasphemy, which many people won't forgive them for. In breaking the rules, these people prove they exist in the first place. And we all know that the messenger is often the first one to get shot.

Parents, predominantly, are the gatekeepers of gender expression in their offspring. Whether we're reluctant to take up this role or not, we become the gender judges who say 'yes' or 'no' to our child's gender style. From clothing through to toys, vocabulary, friendships,

5   Fine, C. (2010) *Delusions of Gender: The Real Science Behind Sex Differences.* London: Icon Books.

play activities, books and screen preferences, we get to decide what's acceptable or not, and almost exclusively so in our children's early years. Through multiple interactions and feedback loops, actively and passively, verbally and non-verbally we, as the adults around the child, teach gender as a main subject. Gradually these transmissions will sketch an outline in the child's developing psyche, which biology and culture will, in time, colour in. These messages can be subtle yet powerfully conveyed by only a sigh, for instance, or blatantly explicit as I witnessed last week in my local café.

I was quietly looking over notes for this book, tucked into a corner and enjoying the mid-morning lull before the lunch-time rush hour. There were a couple of spaces left at my table and before long a man asked if he could join me. As soon as he did, I could feel he was keen to make conversation, and I was keen to avoid it. I scribbled away, hoping he'd take the hint and pick up the paper he'd brought into the café with him. He didn't. As he waited for his breakfast, he suddenly announced he was looking after his 15-month-old son that night. He had no idea what my notes were about, so his comment struck me as synchronistic and I looked up. Spurred on by my attention, he proceeded to tell me that he had three other children and this one was still breastfeeding. His frown said it all. I commiserated with him and asked if the mother had been expressing milk so the baby could be bottle-fed? He replied with a flick of his hand and a quick grin, 'No, we're not bothering with all that. He's just going to have to man-up and live without it.' As I raised my eyebrows and picked my pen back up, I wondered if the parents would subject a girl infant to such harsh emotional cold-turkey? Probably not. Either way, it seems they were about to impress, on their son's susceptible psyche, a lesson in what being a boy supposedly means.

We know gender identity is assimilated in multiple ways, including through colour coding, how we use language, parent feedback and peer pressure. Adults, generally, orchestrate this process, whether we're aware of it or not. Social psychologists, for instance, stress the significance of observational learning; where children model the behaviour of those around them and the influence this has on their gender formation. They also highlight the possibility of parents teaching gender through operant conditioning. Simply put, behaviours that lead to positive consequences for the child are more likely to be repeated than those that don't. What this might look like day to day is a parent complimenting a daughter when she's wearing a 'pretty' dress instead of her customary jeans and boots, or parents proudly supporting their son's athletic prowess while remaining antagonistic towards his ambition to become a dancer. Through these subtle and not-so-subtle signals, it's argued, we coach our children in a million and one ways as to what being a girl, or being a boy, must mean.

The extent to which adults treat children differently according to their sex is full of contradiction and complexity. There's evidence to suggest, for instance, that gendered expectations influence mothers' perceptions of their child's physical abilities, believing a boy infant to be more advanced than a girl.[6] Then there's the research that seems to confirm that a girl infant benefits from greater warmth, patience and concern.[7] By the toddler and pre-school years, some research indicates that mothers talk more to girls than to boys and they speak differently about emotions to the two sexes.[8] The evidence for and against how parents and caregivers influence both the meaning and performance of gender remains inconclusive. What is irrefutable, however, is that ultimately children pay the social cost when there's any significant deviation from the norm.

In 1991, two researchers, Lytton and Romney, conducted a meta-analysis of studies that looked at the parental treatment of girls and

---

6   Fine, C. (2010) *Delusions of Gender: The Real Science Behind Sex Differences.* London: Icon Books, p.204.

7   Fine, C. (2010) *Delusions of Gender: The Real Science Behind Sex Differences.* London: Icon Books, p.198.

8   Fine, C. (2010) *Delusions of Gender: The Real Science Behind Sex Differences.* London: Icon Books, p.199.

boys. They were concerned that the bulk of research largely focused on mothers with children under six and overlooked fathers. The study included 27,836 participants from 158 studies in North America and 17 in other Western countries. Their analysis concluded that, in many ways, parents treated their children more or less the same. There was negligible evidence that, in terms of interaction, communication and warmth, sons and daughters were responded to differently. But there was one striking exception: parents promoted gender-typed play and activities and discouraged cross-gender behaviour.[9]

Play matters

Play matters. It's a serious business that fulfils many functions in the development of any child. When we're around kids in full play flow it's often delightful, and it's also self-evident how hard they work at what they're doing. Children engage and interact with the world around them through their creativity and this has a direct bearing on brain development. That's why they need access to a wide variety of toys and play experience to increase their repertoire of knowledge and skills, be they physical, emotional or social. When we limit children's choices, we limit their development. The consequences of this are far-reaching, and very serious indeed:

> Research shows that children's interests, ambitions, and skills can be shaped early on by the media they consume and the toys with which they play, potentially influencing everything from the subjects they choose to study to the careers they ultimately pursue. Consequently, these early experiences can affect not just

9   Lytton, H. and Romney, D. M. (1991) ' Parents' differential socialization of boys and girls: A meta-analysis.' *Psychological Bulletin 109* (2) 267–96.

their development and life choices, but the composition of our workforce and the strength of our economy for decades to come.[10]

These words are taken from the fact sheet that accompanied the 2016 White House conference, 'Helping Our Children Explore, Learn, and Dream Without Limits: Breaking Down Gender Stereotypes in Media and Toys'. The briefing makes the following point:

> STEM (Science, Technology, Engineering and Math) industries offer some of the highest-paying, most in-demand careers – there are over 600,000 unfilled jobs in information technology alone – yet women hold only 29 percent of STEM jobs. Communities across America are also experiencing teacher shortages, and nursing is one of the fastest-growing professions – yet fewer than 25 percent of public school teachers and only 9 percent of nurses are men.[11]

In many ways perhaps it isn't so complicated after all is it? A=B=C. When we insist on gender conformity over the freedom to be creative, when we marshal kids into gender boxes and rap their tender knuckles if they stray, when we tease and shame children for being different to how they're 'supposed' to be, then diversity is lost; the human eco-system evolves out of synch and, without diversity, the life blood of creativity gradually seeps away.

10   Office of the Press Secretary (2016) *Breaking Down Gender Stereotypes in Media and Toys so that Our Children Can Explore, Learn, and Dream without Limits*. Washington: The White House.
11   Office of the Press Secretary (2016) *Breaking Down Gender Stereotypes in Media and Toys so that Our Children Can Explore, Learn, and Dream without Limits*. Washington: The White House.

Once upon a time...

For the last half-century, toys, entertainment and retail have both reacted to demand and contrived a market that's been characterised by gender stereotyping. Brands have been built, unashamedly, on the binary, and the financial rewards have been astronomical in some cases. The impact of this gender propaganda has been inescapable. Anyone who spends money on gifts for children will have been confronted by this stark reality. The blue and pink badge of group identity is imprinted everywhere, from shampoo bottles to shoelaces. Toys that reinforce action and innovation for boys, and intimacy and attractiveness for girls, are still positioned centre stage. Even the shift away from Barbie and Action Man towards princesses and superheroes still represents far-fetched femininity and overblown masculinity, only this time in the shiny 'celebrity' context of the 21st century. And the labelling, display and advertising of these products all affect customers' buying habits, be they child or adult. The Matrix is so dominant in this arena, it almost eclipses the centrality of one fact: all toys are gender neutral; it's the marketing of them that isn't. But this wall-to-wall gender monopoly is being challenged. In the last decade or so, parents, teachers and other concerned adults have been pushing back, and pushing back hard.

'Let Toys Be Toys', a parent-led campaign that grew out of a thread on the United Kingdom's most popular website, Mumsnet, has become an award-winning project. Its mission is simple: 'We're asking retailers, booksellers and manufacturers to sort and label toys and books by theme or function, rather than by gender, and let the children decide which toys they enjoy best.'[12] To date, 14 outlets including major UK retail players such as Marks & Spencer, Debenhams and Boots, have made changes or have promised to do so. In 2013 the campaign launched a 'Toymark good practice award

---

12   See http://lettoysbetoys.org.uk.

scheme', which recognises and promotes book and toy retailers that are marketing their products inclusively to all children. Currently, 50 companies have been publicly acknowledged in this way for doing so. On a macro level there's the suggestion of a sea-change, with multinational retail companies such as Target and Amazon revising their gender-based categories at the beck of parent power.[13] It hasn't all been plain sailing, yet the tide of opposition refusing to accept the segregation of children's experience by gender continues to rise. Corporations, be they deeply sincere in their efforts or cynical in their revisions, are not exempt from the winds of cultural change. The Walt Disney Company, constructed entirely on the fantasy of childhood innocence, is no exception. Analysis of their animated films demonstrates how, in the classic era of *Snow White* and *Cinderella*, 83 per cent of compliments paid to female characters related to their appearance and, by 2013, this had reduced to 31 per cent. Similarly, compliments related to the skills of female characters averaged around 13 per cent in *Cinderella* and *Sleeping Beauty*, and peaked, two generations, later at 56 per cent in *Brave*, dropping to 35 per cent in *Frozen*.[14, 15] In recent times, Disney, at almost 100 years old itself, has come under criticism for both its reluctance to include any LGBTQ characters and its parodying of them, despite this. Damian Alexander makes it clear why this is not acceptable: 'When children watch entertainment that tells them that people like themselves are

13   Tabuchi, H. (2015) 'Sweeping away gender-specific toys and labels.' *New York Times*, 27 October. Available at www.nytimes.com/2015/10/28/business/sweeping-away-gender-specific-toys-and-labels.html, accessed on 22 July 2017.

14   'Gender Revolution' (2017) *National Geographic Magazine* (special issue, January 2017). Available at www.nationalgeographic.com/magazine/2017/01, accessed on 14 July 2017.

15   Andrew Solomon makes the salient point: 'In an age when women can work in construction and men can marry men, the notion of a medically enshrined, "Batman v. Snow White" typology of gender identity seems reductive, yet it still has considerable currency in the medical literature'. Solomon, A. (2014) *Far From the Tree: Parents, Children and the Search for Identity*. London: Penguin Random House, p.606.

non-heroic, marginal, or villainous, they begin to feel that maybe the TV's right.'[16]

The neuroscientist Cordelia Fine, in *Delusions of Gender: The Real Science Behind Sex Difference*, expertly draws on a mesmerising range of sources to make her case: 'Our minds, society and neurosexism create difference. Together they wire gender. But the wiring is soft, not hard. It is flexible, malleable and changeable. And, if we only believe this it will continue to unravel.'[17] Fine's research is extensive and her analysis incisive. She has this to say about the difficult place our children find themselves in ('…born into a half-changed world, to parents with half-changed minds'[18]):

> Some parents, at least, genuinely want to rear children outside the constraints of rigid stereotypes…they sincerely believe that boys and girls deserve to be free to develop their own interests and to become rounded individuals – gender norms be damned – yet at the same time they channel and craft their children's 'gender performance', especially for boys.[19]

I can relate to this. While I aspired to be gender neutral in my grandparenting role, I was under no illusion that I was. But I never reckoned on the speed with which my perceptions governed my thoughts and behaviour. On an everyday level I believed I was accepting of my family's situation, then there would be a 'trigger' event and a gap would open up inside of me. This gap, between my

16   Alexander, D. (2015) *Get with the Program: The Coming Out of Children's Cartoons.* Available at https://psmag.com/get-with-the-program-the-coming-out-of-children-s-cartoons-da28cdcof349#.hlsqmkjrm, accessed on 22 July 2017.

17   Fine, C. (2010) *Delusions of Gender: The Real Science Behind Sex Differences.* London: Icon Books, p.239.

18   Fine, C. (2010) *Delusions of Gender: The Real Science Behind Sex Differences.* London: Icon Books, p.xxviii.

19   Fine, C. (2010) *Delusions of Gender: The Real Science Behind Sex Differences.* London: Icon Books, p.204.

thoughts and my feelings, showed me I wasn't as fine as I thought I was. Psychologists call this 'cognitive dissonance'. As Ruben began to bridge the world between his assigned and affirmed gender, I fell through this space repeatedly. I remember, in particular, one spring morning when Jude called to say that Ruben, for the first time, would be wearing girl's clothes for the day and they would soon be calling round. I reasoned away a stubborn crease of uneasiness as she spoke to me: I was used to seeing Ruben in his 'princess gowns' and this probably wouldn't be so different, I told myself. But when they arrived and I saw Ruben getting out of the car, tears pressed against my eyes and I felt unable to swallow. Even though I loved this child fervently, what I instinctively registered was something between profound incongruity and utter dismay. For a moment, all I could see was my grandson in a girl's dress. My initiation as a grandmother transcended my imagination at that point. I yearned, simply, for all to be as it once was. Much later on, after the lunch dishes were cleared and my daughter was getting ready to leave, Ruben sat at my table colouring in a self-portrait. His legs were swinging beneath his silver skirts and his pale blue cardigan was folded next to mine on the chair. Then I only saw my little one. Happy. Safe. At his nanny's and campaigning to stay the night.

As we now move towards the hinterland of the Matrix, you will notice one thing in particular, if you haven't noticed it already: when you chisel into the concrete frame holding gender in place, other frames of reference you have may begin to crack too. The fact is, when we begin to deconstruct one difference that is maligned culturally, we inevitably educate ourselves about other differences too. Your experience of defending your child against questioning scowls or disapproving words may be another person's because their child has mental health struggles, a mixed-heritage parentage, is on the autistic spectrum or presents as androgynous. Do you see where I'm going here? Culture, and consensus reality, is only ever a made-up thing.

CHAPTER 5

MAINTAINING THE MATRIX

Being part of the in-crowd

Each of us has a personal experience of gender we live every day of our lives. Most people identify as either male or female and behave, dress and interact with others accordingly. Our gender experience 'just feels normal' and we frequently assume everyone else feels the same way about themselves too. Rarely do we question when and how we learnt to feel this way. But what if you decide to drastically alter something about your gender identity overnight? If you deliberately go against the gender grain you've conformed to up until now? Perhaps as a woman you spend the duration of an office meeting with your legs astride and your hands behind your head? Or as a man you wear coral nail varnish and apricot lip gloss into work? One thing can be predicted, things will change in some way. The expression of your new-found difference will ensure that. If your gender variance proves significant enough, people in the street might stare or direct comments towards you. Anonymous drivers might jeer out of their car windows and shop assistants avoid eye contact when you ask them a question. Or someone might feel compelled to tell you that you're brave. Suddenly, the gender cover you didn't know you'd taken for granted will be blown away, and you'll feel exposed. But exposed as what? Or to whom?

As members of mainstream groups, such as heterosexuals or cisgender people, we fail to recognise how society is biased in our favour. This isn't surprising, because when we comply with prescribed 'boxes' we're consistently rewarded for being 'normal'. Feeling normal comes about when aspects of who we intrinsically are, such as our skin colour, sexuality and gender, go unquestioned as a matter of course in our daily lives. This results in us being able to forget about them. And, subsequently, this translates into solid social capital when it comes to engaging with the culture at large. For instance, I recently had to attend a hospital appointment for an investigation of my upper chest area. I wasn't looking forward to the endoscopy, as you can imagine. When I got to the hospital the consultant had read my notes and he put me at ease, asking some general questions about my lifestyle. There were several nurses in the room, and one was designated to hold my hand as the procedure got underway, which he did with some warmth. Thankfully, there was nothing serious amiss and I quickly recovered from the discomfort I'd experienced. Initially I thought nothing more of this experience until I began to think about it in the light of unearned cisgender benefits. So what were they? First, I could rest assured that the consultant, or any other of the hospital staff, wouldn't question the pronouns I use or the validity of the formal documents I had brought with me. Secondly, no-one suggested or assumed that the medical issue I presented with was a result of my gender. I didn't have to anticipate any intrusive questioning based on my gender identity being seen as a mental disorder and classified as such. Thirdly, I didn't have to prepare myself to be treated as confused, misled or simply strange. I could expect a professional service and receive one, not least from the nurse who helped me to feel relaxed throughout an unpleasant procedure. And lastly, I could have some confidence that the healthcare I received wasn't hampered by personal judgements and covert prejudice.[1]

Until I reflected on this experience more closely, I understood it to be no more than my right as a UK tax-paying citizen to receive

---

1   These reflections and insights are, obviously, limited by the confines of my own experience as a cisgender woman. I've no doubt that the experience I'm only imagining can be far more subtle, layered, diminishing and unpredictable.

this standard of care, along with 'everyone else'. But everyone else isn't me and everyone else doesn't tick as many boxes as I do. The research, reading and meetings I've engaged in for this book have now facilitated an entirely different scale to measure my experience against. As I did so, I began to discern how much of my treatment at the hospital I simply took for granted, and on what grounds this was made possible. I saw how potential barriers existed for other people that I've never needed to consider. Finally, I recognised how many of the benefits I normally enjoy blend into the background of my life because I've come to expect them, when, in fact, a significant number of them are contingent on my group membership. There's a danger looming here when we confuse one with the other. We can assume, and mostly do, that our right to something is being upheld because of who we are individually, and not because of our group fraternity. If we remain unaware of this, another risk emerges: we may well develop a subtle sense of superiority. This manifests in our expectations that we should be served first, that others should speak our native tongue to us, that the dropdown box on the computer should put our country of residence at the top of the list, that someone should make the time to see us, that our 'requests' are, in fact, actually demands and, that we know what's best for other people. When we occupy a mainstream position, the likelihood of subtle, unhealthy entitlement traits increases. The renowned peace activist Thich Nhat Hanh gives this advice: 'Every thought you produce, anything you say, any action you do, it bears your signature.'[2] These wise words give us cause to pause and reflect, and may perhaps influence us to do some things differently.

The passports we have to the groups we belong to invite us into other ones because like attracts like. Over time, we discover that major benefits begin to multiply as a result of these partnerships. We earn 'interest' as we network and interact with other in-groups

2   Hanh, T. N. (1995) *Peace Is Every Step: The Path of Mindfulness in Everyday Life.* London: Ebury Publishing. Also available at www.brainyquote.com/citation/ quotes/quotes/t/thichnhath531603.html, accessed on 01 September 2017.

that validate our own. As we both invest in and reward each other, a tight relationship is woven that yields rich dividends. These include, though aren't limited to, robust legal rights, educational resources, employment opportunities, appropriate healthcare and good prospects for a high quality of life. Going about one's daily life with the sense of freedom that 'feeling normal' gives you is an astonishing privilege. From this lofty position we don't have to continually assess risk in our environments or query why people may be treating us differently to someone else. And, significantly, the systems and structures we make use of every day, will be shaped around our needs. What we harvest from all of this is a profound sense of psychological, emotional and physical safety, simply because we're part of the in-crowd.

Most of us have been taught about social disadvantage; few of us have been taught to think about how we might be over-privileged as a result of it. Invariably, if this taboo is questioned, it will be shut down using two clamps of steel: silence and denial. These clamps crush any possibility of honest debate because they shield advantage and promote the system that creates it. When we're part of powerful mainstream groups, more often than not we have no idea about the extent of our privilege. This comes about because we're not schooled in understanding there are conditions to our membership. We assume entry is free.

Your mind creates your world...

So what is it that that drives us to include some people and exclude others with such zeal? Why do we, as a species, behave this way? Why does what's 'true' change its meaning from place to place, and viewpoints differ in the same situation? Our perceptions – or as we can also call them, our frames of reference – are responsible for this. How we see and interpret things determines our attitude and behaviours in response. In this way our mind truly does create our world. Our perceptions are not, after all, undisputed facts about reality and who we share it with.

Only this weekend I was reading in a British newspaper how a patient's learning disability was cited as one reason to activate a 'do not resuscitate' order if he developed heart or breathing problems in hospital.[3] So what was happening here? How come a group of professionals, devoted to saving lives, made a judgement that this man's life was less worthy of saving because of a learning disability? We can only judge something in comparison to something else. It seems that the doctors had placed their patient next to an able-bodied person in their collective imagination and found him wanting. If we adopt a 'big picture' view of this situation, it's possible to see the layers of privilege, value judgements and prejudice knotted through it. The backdrop is the historical context of medical elitism, the script that the doctor 'always knows best'. The patient, who has Down's syndrome, represents the 'disabled' out-group, and the doctors the powerful 'able-bodied' in-group. In the mix too is a nurse who challenged the medics several times and was persistently ignored. She was aware that the doctors had failed to consult with the man's relatives about the instruction, even though this was a requirement. The nurse, called an ally by any other name, finally informed the patient's family who subsequently took legal action to protect their loved one's rights. The ensuing tribunal upheld her actions and the family's complaint. If it wasn't for the integrity and bravery of the nurse, the professional with the *least* power in the situation, this situation could have cost the man his life and his family would have been bereaved unnecessarily.[4]

The forces that condition our minds are formidable: family, religion, economic class, education, 'race', gender, cultural expectations and norms, to name only a few primary sources. This is true for the

---

3   Gayle, D. (2015) 'Hospital says sorry for do not resuscitate order on man with Down's syndrome.' *The Guardian*, 8 December.

4   In the United Kingdom, a lack of intention to discriminate against a person is no defence in law.

doctors I refer to above, and for you and me. There are no exceptions. We breathe these influences in, just as a plant absorbs all the elements in its environment. It's impossible not to. Ultimately, these influences form an intricate filigree over our psyches and in our bodies, which we, as human beings, then breathe the world through. So none of us actually ever see the world as *it is*, we only ever see it as *we are*. The filigree will change over time, although the extent to which it does is influenced by many factors, not least how available we are to new experiences and all they can add to our lives.

I once attended a pioneering conference about diversity. There were close to 400 delegates in the London venue, representing more than 40 countries, and we were together for five full days. The emotional temperature ranged from simmering to searing as the week went on with very little else in-between. During one session, when people were being invited to step forward and express their grievances, I became frustrated by the apparent reticence of one eloquent man to do so. He was an Aboriginal person and I'd heard him speaking over lunch about the depth of discrimination his community suffered. He was standing at the very back of the large ballroom and I was standing with a close friend, a black woman from the United Kingdom. I couldn't understand why he failed to step forward and expressed this to my friend. I expected a nod of her head and a deep sigh of agreement. Instead I was met with silence and a piercing look, which she fixed on me like a laser. Later that day, confused, I asked her to give me some feedback because her response had confounded me. After 30 fractious minutes or so, striving to stay open and undefended, I fathomed the source of my friend's indignity. My frustration was a mirror of my unconscious white advantage. Why? Because all I'd seen was a man shying away from a positive opportunity to act. And, not only that, I'd judged this action both ignorantly and harshly. In fact, I'd failed to recognise, entirely, that my racial identity had always been my passport to privilege, whereas this man's had been tantamount to an arrest warrant.

The consensus reality each of us experienced was radically divergent. In my crude assessment, I'd applied the same rules of engagement to us both as though our experience in the world was equal. My friend comprehended this in a way I couldn't at the time. I had privilege written on my skin, and both she and the Aboriginal man did not. My friend's anger and my willingness to hear and learn from it took apart and reconfigured a part of the filigree I was looking through at the world. The following day, when the Aboriginal leader stepped into the centre of the room and picked up the microphone, I was able to see with new eyes. Here was a dignified man, standing in the hot ashes of colonialism, turning his face toward racism, cultural devastation and unspeakable trauma. What courage it took to risk his terrible truth. To speak, in the full knowledge that he might well be misunderstood, or even attacked, for doing so.

I had several 'paradigm shifts' over the conference – a fundamental change in my approach and assumptions – and all of them were equally uncomfortable in their own way. Challenging our perceptions is a very hard thing to do. How we see the world is absolutely critical to who we believe ourselves to be. So when we find the guts to allow perceptions that no longer serve us to fall away, it's akin to paring away parts of our identity. It can hurt. I've come to welcome this suffering as a necessary part of growth. I know it will pass. A plant that is pot-bound must first endure a rough separation from its captor before it can freely develop again. So it is for humans. We're uniquely placed to challenge and alter our perceptions through a willingness to be open, to consciously reflect, struggle and resource ourselves to think 'outside of the box'.

Being part of the out-crowd

Instead of taking for granted the freedom that feeling normal gives you, imagine the opposite experience is true. Imagine that you find yourself in an out-group. Many of us will know how this experience can feel: the way our body seems to take up less space, how time seems to mock us, the way we fantasise about 'hitting back' or find ourselves scanning the room for a sympathetic glance. When the out-group experience is a negative one, it can take quite some time to get over. Thankfully, for the great majority of us it's a temporary experience we can usually walk away from. But what happens when a permanent aspect of your identity gets fed back to you, again and again, as odd, inferior or even contaminated? When, in most situations, every day, you're perceived as being part of the out-crowd? Who amongst us could escape such circumstances unscathed?

As Eva walked towards me in the café we'd arranged to meet in, she reminded me of a 1940s film star, complete with a fake fox fur draped across one of her shoulders. Eva is a 17-year-old trans woman, who's as articulate as she is glamorous. She's also someone who suffered savage bullying for a number of years at school and in the community. Eva's poised outward appearance belies a different internal reality:

I think being numb is my subconscious reaction to not wanting to be here. The best way to not wanting to be here, is to not really feel anything. To have no reaction to it at all and so, I don't know, I think people think they know me a lot more personally than they do because I'm okay with talking about my experiences. Like you, you probably assumed at the start, it would be painful for me to talk about everything, but it's not. I am not gonna keep myself to myself about it. I'm fine with talking because I've closed myself off almost permanently. So I'm not dealing with much. When you cut yourself off to your emotions, you become very helpful to other people. I'm very understanding because I'm not dealing with anything myself. It's very easy to go into someone else's world because my world is empty. I think there's a lot below the surface but the surface is platinum, if you know what I mean. So it's difficult to get there with me.

Eva is a survivor. A remarkable young person. The actions of others, including a senior transphobic teacher who went unchallenged by her peers, have exacted a terrible toll. It's testimony to her fortitude, and the love of her mother, that she's now returned to education and is beginning to trust in a better future for herself.

Shame, if it becomes toxic, is a formidable enemy. When a person feels this sort of shame, it's who they are, not what they do, that becomes the focus of their evaluation. Repeated traumatic experiences are at the core of this. It might be for one person that, within their family, expressing a part of themselves is unacceptable or even forbidden. Each time this negative message is transmitted to them, be it subtle or strong, a brick is laid down in their psyche. Eventually a detention centre is built where this reviled part is held, with no prospect of release. Soon, in its isolation, the part begins to experience itself as despised and despicable. Feelings of worthlessness, powerlessness and self-loathing prevail. And if, as so often is the case, the part that's been shamed is met with hostility in the outer world too, the effect is vice-like. Subsequently, when the person attempts to express this part of themselves in any situation, instead of authenticity they experience a debilitating hit of toxic shame. This terrible double-bind – express oneself and be rejected, or deny oneself and be received – is the wretched situation many people who don't conform to gender norms find themselves in. Andrew Solomon elegantly puts it thus: 'A double life is exhausting and ultimately tragic, because you can't ever be loved if you can never be known.'[5]

It's no secret that children and young people who are gender expansive are at greater risk of mental health difficulties than those who are not. The Gay, Lesbian and Straight Education Network

---

5   Solomon, A. (2014) *Far from the Tree: Parents, Children and the Search for Identity.* London: Penguin Random House, p.622.

(GLSEN) *2015 National School Climate Survey*[6] may help us to understand why. The survey found that 54.5 per cent of children and young people experienced verbal abuse in relation to their gender expression, 20.3 per cent physical harassment and 9.4 per cent physical assault; 56 per cent didn't report the violence and harassment and, of those that did, 63.5 per cent said staff did nothing about it. These statistics relate to gender expression alone and not sexual orientation or transgender experience, where abuse was more prevalent. They make for distressing reading because, as we all know, when the world affirms our belonging and worth to us, life is easier.

This is not the whole picture though and for that I offer gratitude. It seems, at least in some parts of the world, that affirmation is increasing where little existed before. The *2015 U.S. Transgender Survey*, which an unprecedented number – nearly 28,000 – gender-diverse people participated in, revealed the following:

> Despite the undeniable hardships faced by transgender people, respondents' experiences also show some of the positive impacts of growing visibility and acceptance of transgender people in the United States... Respondents' experiences also suggest growing acceptance by family members, colleagues, classmates, and other people in their lives... More than two-thirds (68%) of those who were out to their co-workers reported that their co-workers were supportive. Of students who were out to their classmates, more than half (56%) reported that their classmates supported them as a transgender person.[7]

6   GLSEN (2015) *2015 National School Climate Survey – Executive Summary*. Available at www.glsen.org/sites/default/files/GLSEN%202015%20National%20School%20 Climate%20Survey%20%28NSCS%29%20-%20Executive%20Summary.pdf, accessed on 14 July 2017.

7   National Center of Transgender Equality (2016) *2015 U.S. Transgender Survey*, p.4.

Nickie, whom we met earlier grappling with her mum, Zoe, about wearing a bra to school, is one such student. Nickie's 'tomboy' identity gradually evolved into a binary transgender identity when he was 15:

> I was really lucky in having friends that were accepting of me either way. Some people in my school were aware of it and tried to make fun of me, but I was never really persecuted. I just kind of felt that I had my mates and I knew who I was on good terms with and who was cool with me. People who were annoying me, they'd make me angry, we sometimes had fights, but at the end of the day it was alright because I had friends and family. I remember the first teacher I did tell, she wasn't really a teacher, she was a pastoral worker. Everyone called her the mum of the school because she was really nice and friendly. I was really nervous about what she was going to say. I told her, 'I'm trans,' and she was like, she gave me a hug, she was like, 'I'm glad that you've finally realised, and you're getting closer to being that person.' And she asked if I wanted to tell everyone else or keep it between us. And the fact that she asked, that was really nice. She's all about confidentiality, so if you don't want to tell someone, unless you're in danger, she's cool with that. And I said, 'If you want to tell them, yes.' So she did tell the other teachers and they were fine with it.

It's clear from everything that Nickie shared with me, that the pastoral worker, and the school in general, signalled safety to him throughout his time there. The school has a zero-tolerance policy with regard to bullying, and positively welcome diversity. The staff worked closely with Zoe to ensure Nickie's personal needs as well as educational ones were met. Nickie is fortunate – he's grown up in a home where safety signals are also explicit. The night his step-sister came out to their parents as lesbian, and her girlfriend was welcomed into their home, was the night Nickie decided to declare his identity to the family, too. Zoe rolled her eyes and shook her head with a smile when she told me about it:

> They're as thick as thieves those two. They talk a lot and it obviously got Nickie thinking about it. She wrote me a letter and brought it down to us. A beautiful fucking letter and when she says the word 'transgender', she wrote it in big letters with big things coming out of it. Like, this is it. She gave us the letter and said to us, just read this and think about it and talk to me later about it. I read it, and it was like, a proper night of revelations.

Being part of an out-crowd can be a devastating ordeal, though this is by no means a foregone conclusion, as Nickie's story shows us. One researcher on identity puts it this way: 'Discrimination might be an everyday event, but it is no longer an all-day event.'[8]

An out-group experience can catapult people into a sense of 'rightness' about who they are. Surviving adversity can build a fortress sense of identity, based on an internal freedom that can't be touched. I want to honour the families and communities who work to support and empower this. I want to broadcast the courage, integrity, determination, passion and faith that many, many gender-expansive children and young people manifest. And I want to offer solace to us as parents and caregivers. We are navigating a treacherous path: we must do everything in our power to protect our child, while simultaneously refusing to project onto them, the identity of a victim.

8   Fanshawe, S. and Sriskandarajah, D. (2010) 'You can't put me in a box: Super-diversity and the end of identity politics in Britain.' Institute for Public Policy Research (IPPR), p.7. Available at www.ippr.org/publications/you-cant-put-me-in-a-box-super-diversity-and-the-end-of-identity-politics-in-britain, accessed on 14 July 2017.

Attuning to the world of your child

When we attune to the world of our child, it means that we're able to imaginatively, and empathically, assess what's going on for them. Our logic, feelings and intuition must flow together to achieve this effectively. Through it a child learns that they have an inner life, and this realisation is the precursor to appreciating that other people have inner lives too. Effective attunement leads to trust. You know a great deal about this process already. When your little one was barely days old, you already began to develop an instinct about whether they were hungry, had wind in their tummy or needed a nap. A few weeks later you could pick their cry out of a room full of other infants who might also be grizzling. Later on, you learnt how to interpret your child's sounds; you recognised they were feeling frustrated as you listened to them through the kitchen window. You went outside and showed them how to manoeuvre a toy truck down the garden path. You didn't laugh when they cried because they'd ran over a snail. Then there were the many times you checked under the bed for something sinister and promised them you'd keep the light on until they fell asleep. Or understood in your teenager's tantrums that, really, they were simply exhausted from learning how to grow up, and just needed a break.

In essence, attunement is both instinct and learned behaviour: it's the capacity to both tune into and then accurately interpret the non-verbal and verbal clues our children give us about what's going on in their inner world. When a parent is able to do this well enough, and meets the identified needs, an infant will thrive. Through repeated experiences of this cycle, a child comes to understand, at a core cellular level, that the world is safe. And, most critically, they know who, and where, to return to if this proves not to be the case.

Lewis and Gina, a young couple who live in a green corner of Birmingham, a sprawling city in the United Kingdom, have two daughters. Their eldest, Andi, is a sensitive six-year-old who was assigned male at birth, though transitioned socially several months before we met. All has gone well and the school has been exceptionally supportive. As Gina told me, 'If there's any teasing or anything else going on, the school are on it before we even hear about it. The head teacher is really committed to equality, thank goodness.' Thank goodness indeed. Lewis and Gina keep a close eye on Andi because they know that she strongly internalises her feelings, and can struggle to articulate them. Sometimes this results in unexpected bursts of emotion. Lewis, who shares all the childcare with his partner, told me about a recent outburst when he and Andi were at home together. They'd had a busy, though relaxed, day and it was drawing towards bedtime. Lewis noticed that Andi seemed subdued and first of all assumed she was just tired. Then, over dinner, Andi was moody and irritable with her sister and wouldn't eat her meal. Instead of 'just jumping in', Lewis asked her instead if anything was the matter. Andi burst into tears and sobbed, 'One day I'm going to have hair on my face, aren't I? Aren't I? And no-one can do anything about it.'

Lewis was, once again, shocked by the intensity, and the unfairness, of the world his little one has to inhabit. He and Gina had never discussed hormone blockers with their daughter, and assumed they wouldn't need to until she was a few years older. Lewis had to make a split-second decision on his own:

> I could have pacified her with a superficial comment like 'Don't worry, we're going to take care of that when it happens,' but she needed more than that. She needed to feel safe at a much deeper level than that. So I told her about hormones and how they worked and that Mummy and I have already thought this through, and we're going to sort it all out for her. And do you know what she said to me then? *Daddy, but what if you forget to give them to me?* I told her, I'm your daddy and it's my job to look after you properly. Don't ever forget that, okay? I will remember to give them to you, I promise. You don't have to worry about that, Andi. You don't have to worry at all.

Lewis and Gina are aware and sensitive parents who understand that their daughter has particular needs they must stay attuned to. In a million and one ways you too can practise how to see the world through your child's eyes, in the everydayness of parenting.

As ever, depending on your child's gender web, your specific circumstances and the social context you find yourself in, this will require different things from you at different times. There is no textbook sequence to the gender exploration your youngster has embarked on. Skilful, consistent attunement is your best guide to accepting, understanding and interpreting it. Often, professional help will enhance and unpack this further, as long as it's based on a partnership model with the child's well-being at the heart of it. In essence, everyone must be prepared to 'watch and wait', while at the same time being prepared to 'listen and act' in response to the child's expertise regarding their own needs.[9]

Trust in the Four Keys – listening, imagination, empathy and courage – to equip you to deal with whatever situation you find yourself in. Commit to stretching. Behaviour is a language. How you respond to your child's signals will either build or diminish trust in your relationship. There is no question that our experiences do limit our perception, but our will to learn, understand, empathise and act can change it. What a gift. In other words, we can choose to develop, expand and connect. We can choose to witness our child's journey from their perspective, as well as our own.

Before we move on, let's recap because this is tricky territory that most of us haven't spent much time on. We've been exploring:

- what being part of the in-crowd means

---

9   For a full discussion of this demanding balancing act, see the following: Ehrensaft, D. (2016) *The Gender Creative Child: Pathways for Nurturing and Supporting Children Who Live Outside Gender Boxes*. New York, NY: The Experiment, LLC, pp.158–67. See also: Ehrensaft, D. (2011) *Gender Born, Gender Made*. New York, NY: Experiment, LLC, pp.65–7.

- how this allows us to feel 'normal' because key parts of our identity go unquestioned as a matter of course
- how this results in us being able to forget about them because our 'sameness', not our 'difference', is constantly being reinforced
- how, as such, we don't need to continually risk-assess in our environments or assimilate to feel safe
- how there are many powerful mainstream groups in society: cisgender, heterosexual, male, able-bodied, white-skinned, well-educated, to name only a few
- how the structures around such groups meet our needs if we're members of them
- how, invariably, we fail to recognise this and assume that these are individual 'rights' and not contingent on our group membership
- how, as such, we can personally assume 'entitlement traits', which influence our thoughts, feelings and behaviours.

We've also been exploring:

- what being part of the out-crowd means
- how this gets communicated when a permanent part of identity routinely gets fed back as 'abnormal' or contaminated
- how LGBTQ children and young people are targeted in this way
- how visibility and acceptance of transgender people is improving
- how accepting family and friends create good mental-health outcomes
- how being part of a non-mainstream group can be an enriching experience.

And, finally, we've been exploring:

- how our mind creates our world
- how powerful social and cultural forces shape and sustain our perceptions
- how our experience of reality is mediated through this filter
- how a willingness to be open, to consciously reflect and struggle, will enable us to 'think outside of the box'
- how our perception and engagement with 'difference' will change accordingly
- how the natural process of attunement, practised consciously, will enable us to 'tune in' to the inner world of our gender-expansive child
- how this will create in them a profound sense of safety and security within our relationship.

It's clear when we survey the lists above that the convergence of multiple elements, individually and collectively, conspire to maintain the Gender Matrix. Identifying them is the first step in unmasking what binds them together.

CHAPTER 6

UNMASKING THE MATRIX

Power, privilege, rank

To become an effective ally is to become conversant with power: our own, other people's and that which institutions trade on. Talking out loud about power is something many of us feel uncomfortable about doing. In many ways it's a taboo subject we creep around or enjoy vicariously through films, books and playing online games. Yet we all know what it feels like to be powerful and to feel powerless. We know what it feels like to be 'put down' and to behave in controlling and dominating ways.

Power can be defined as the ability people have to achieve their purposes, whatever their purposes happen to be. And people will exercise this ability in radically different ways. Power, overwhelmingly, has had bad press because we associate it, very often, with abuse. And, as we've already seen, abuse has far-reaching and devastating consequences in people's lives. This repels most of us and it's one reason we draw back from really engaging with the subject. As allies to gender-expansive kids, we can't afford this luxury anymore; we must come into a healthy relationship with power or, inevitably, our children will suffer. This is a hard reality and a necessary one to face up to. The difference our child carries provokes all sorts of responses and reactions, as we know. Some of them are supportive, and many can be unfair or even unfathomable. Without a clear understanding of the dynamics of power, we aren't going to be able to manage or neutralise the impact of such negativity. So let's wade more deeply into the waters of power, rank and privilege now, to swim and not only paddle at the edges of this topic. As I've mentioned before, deconstructing the Gender Matrix gives us the tools to understand how other differences are marginalised in our society, so I'd encourage you to think broadly as you work through this part of the book.

Power 'over'

I remember the moment I realised as a parent that I was exercising power in a way that felt wrong to me. It was a late autumn afternoon, I was bone-tired and my kids were playing up. I was in my early 30s, with four children, and I screeched across the room at the oldest two. I don't recall what I said, only that the words hung in the air long enough for their echo to ring in my ears. I heard them. And I was shocked. As my son and daughter looked at me in silence, I inwardly interrogated myself:

'Would you talk to their father like that?'

'No.'

'Would you talk to your sister like that?'

'No.'

'Would you talk to any of your friends like that?'

'No.'

'Then why are you talking to your children like that?'

The answer was a simple one and it arrived swiftly: 'Because I can.' The answer rocked me. I had power. And if I wasn't prepared to look straight into its teeth, I would end up tearing bloody pieces out of those I loved the most.

Like many people parented in the 1950s and 1960s, I was brought up to the soundtrack of 'Do you want to feel the back of my hand?' A slap across the calves or a thump in the thigh was commonplace. I have an enduring memory of being punched by the headmaster in the side of my skull so hard that I saw stars. I was nine and playfully stepping on the foot of the girl standing next to me while we waited for the morning assembly to start. Adults, generally, felt entitled to hurt children then, whether they were their own or not. Their authority to do so was rarely questioned. I celebrate the huge cultural shift in the last 30 years towards children's rights. I'm tone deaf to the 'Good Old Days' choir and their sad refrain 'It never did me any harm.' I have trouble believing that the frightened child they once were would nod in agreement now. In any other circumstance an adult who slaps, pinches, pushes or punches someone is known as a bully and, sometimes, as a criminal. Why do we frame violence as 'discipline' when it comes to children?

Soon after the personal enquiry this parenting incident initiated in me, another potent experience pinned me to the ground. I had just left my son in reception class and was leaving the school playground as the older children were lining up at the other end of it. I could see their heads bobbing in several rows and the hubbub of their return-to-school energy made me smile. I watched as the deputy head blew a whistle, short and sharp, waited a few moments and took three or four steps towards the nearest child. Then she lunged at her, screaming a tirade, barely a few inches from her face. I was shaking with anger as I left the playground. Yes, *as I left*. I abandoned the terrified child and tormented myself for weeks as to why. I gradually realised how a number of factors had collided within me and driven my reactive behaviour. The teacher's uncontained anger 'triggered' the child in me who had witnessed many episodes of anger like this in my home, so I fled. The teacher's high-ranking status, the fact that our social lives overlapped and all my children were in her school also intimidated me and contributed to my silence. It took me a long time to forgive myself for not challenging this particular abuse of authority. I had to accept, irrespective of my reasons for it that, as an adult, my action was cowardice in the face of *power over*. The only way I knew to redeem the situation was to learn from it. My remorse became fuel to challenge and change myself for the better.

Rank – what does it all mean?

Arnie Mindell, the father of Process Psychology, describes the sum of all of a person's privileges as 'rank'. Process psychologists group rank under four specific headings: social, psychological, spiritual and contextual. We can look at our life through each one of these window panes to gain perspective on the privileges we do, or don't, have:

- **Social:** This includes rank that comes to us through: gender, 'race', age, class, sexual orientation, health, religion, nationality, education, economic status.
- **Psychological:** This includes rank that comes to us through: 'good-enough' attachment to parents and caregivers, having an internal sense of safety, surviving adversity and growing from it, possessing good self-esteem; the capacity to hold personal boundaries, receive positive and critical feedback, and to generate support.
- **Spiritual:** This includes rank that comes to us through: feeling connected to something divine or 'bigger' than human consciousness, a compelling sense of purpose, the certainty of being unconditionally cared for, and deep peace in the core of one's being.
- **Contextual:** This refers to the fluid nature of rank as a whole. Rank isn't static; it's context-dependent, so it ebbs and flows.

You've probably noticed as you made your way through this list, that some of the privileges you've earned, and many of them you just got lucky with. What's important to understand is that rank, in and of itself, isn't wrong in any way. It's what we do with it that counts. When I look through these window panes now, to the Aboriginal man I referenced in Chapter 5, I see that my initial attitude towards him revealed my unconscious privilege and entitlement as a white woman who has never personally experienced pervasive racism. Even though this was unintentional on my part, it could have caused considerable harm if, for instance, I'd argued with my friend or challenged the man directly; or, for that matter, left the conference with my confident judgement intact as the 'truth'. Similarly, the medics who discriminated against the disabled patient were acting out of their entitled mentality as able-bodied professionals who were imbued with authority. In other words, we were both oblivious to the rank we were carrying, and so our perceptions and behaviour arose out of a feeling of superiority that, somehow, we 'knew best'. For myself, joining all of this up felt liberating. This isn't to say that my ego wasn't bruised, that I didn't feel exposed and embarrassed – I did. Very much so. What concerned me more though was 'walking my talk'. And once I'd got past the discomfort and accepted the situation with appropriate humility, I could see how this experience might well enhance areas elsewhere in my life. Painfully learning that 'No, I didn't know best in the conference situation' enabled me to question how many other times this must have also been the case; how many times my judgements and opinions were based on assumptions and entitlement and, in fact, only highlighted a lazy attitude to educating myself.

After everything I've been talking about, it might feel counter-intuitive to enjoy and even celebrate the rank you have. Yet that's what Arnie Mindell and his process psychologist colleagues encourage us to do. Feeling guilty about the privileges you have is not a necessary requirement to bring about change in your perceptions, attitudes and behaviour – quite the opposite, in fact. This sort of reactive guilt often leads to paralysis and no constructive action at all. Instead of becoming immobilised through it, we can plough our attention into noticing the rank we have, then commit to use it productively. As Arnie Mindell says so well, 'If you used rank consciously, it's medicine. Otherwise it's poison.'[1]

---

1   Mindell, A. (1995) *Sitting in the Fire*. Portland, Oregon: Lao Tse Press, p.64.

How much have I got and what do I do with it?

Generally, the greater the rank we have, the more we want of it and the less we recognise the advantages it gives us. I recently came across a website article with a very striking title: 'When You're Accustomed to Privilege, Equality Feels like Oppression.'[2] It caught my attention immediately because I know I've been on both sides of this particular table. The author explained that, usually, when someone in a mainstream position is asked to 'move over' or give something up in favour of someone from a non-mainstream group, they feel affronted, outraged and 'picked on' simply because they're not used to this experience. The request might be to do with reorganising a work rota to take account of a person's caring responsibilities, or to revise a term that's considered not respectable now. Either way, the aggrieved individual will usually go on to rationalise away, minimise or challenge the reasons given for the request to change. These behaviours are all high-rank signals intended to outmanoeuvre the experience of another person or group.

After my experience at the diversity conference, I began to hold the 'rank' lens up to my own life. I was taken aback by the privilege I uncovered. I had no idea it existed in so many corners and corridors of my life. For instance:

- I can travel almost anywhere and someone will speak my first language, English. *Advantage:* I don't have to exercise any effort to be understood or to get my needs met with relative ease.
- I'm articulate and well educated. *Advantage:* I'm not intimidated by bureaucracy and can speak up for my rights.
- I'm able-bodied and healthy. *Advantage:* I can take up any number of social invitations, which impacts favourably on my self-esteem.

---

2   Blog by Chris Boeskool. Available at www.huffingtonpost.com/chris-boeskool/when-youre-accustomed-to-privilege_b_9460662.html, accessed on 22 July 2017.

- I'm psychologically robust. *Advantage:* I'm able to feel positive most of the time and resource myself effectively when I don't.
- I'm cisgender. *Advantage:* I can use a public restroom without the fear of being beaten up, verbally abused or accused of sexual perversion.
- I'm heterosexual. *Advantage:* I can express affection in public spaces freely and don't need to risk assess if it's safe to do so.[3]

Until I understood something about these dynamics, I didn't understand either that rank can be projected onto us, with or without, our wish or consent.

In 2009 I went to Uganda to visit Jude, who was volunteering there at a refugee camp. After spending a fortnight with her, teaching in schools, visiting families, walking so many miles on the baked earth that my ankles hurt, I took a week out to travel to a different part of the country. I soon found myself in the colourful, chaotic bus depot in Kampala, the capital city. The rickety wooden ticket office was boarded shut and I joined a growing gaggle of people waiting for it to open. After an hour it grew to a small crowd. A combination of self-consciousness and English reserve soon meant I'd conceded my place in the throng and moved over to the edges of it. Sweat still rolled off my forehead and down my nose in the midday sun, even though I'd sheltered under the drooping branches of a nearby tree. Eventually, the clattering of boards signalled that the bus tickets were about to go on sale. I recall worrying that they might all be sold by the time I got to the front of the haphazard queue. The burly Ugandan who took his place behind the rickety counter bustled around his desk as he organised his small empire. Then he looked up and out above the heads of every single black person to the one white person in their midst. His pointed finger curled over and beckoned

---

3   As I write this, the news broke yesterday of the massacre in a gay nightclub in Orlando, Florida, on 12 June 2016. What inconsolable grief numerous family members and friends will be waking up to this morning. Their loved ones murdered because they didn't conform to heterosexual 'norms'.

me with a half-closed fist. I have never, in my life, felt so visible. I had no way of understanding if the man's behaviour was sympathetic to a white foreigner, or subservient. I took what felt like a walk of shame through the quiet parted crowd and bought the first ticket. Then I scurried away with beetroot cheeks and found my seat in the front of the empty, waiting bus.

This story also illustrates, perfectly, *contextual rank*, which is when we move from one context to another and realise we're being seen and valued differently. Either way, it's not our mind that first communicates this information to us, it's our body: a lurch in the bowels; a slab of tension landing on the chest; shallow, quick breathing; blushing; laughing; an overwhelming need to stay alert. Depending on the circumstances, these signals flag a positive or negative experience. When our contextual rank shifts, it's highly unlikely that anyone around us will be using terms like 'rank' and 'privilege'. Yet, despite this, in our bones, we all know when we find ourselves 'one down' or in an elevated position.

Rank dynamics are active most of the time. In some situations there's a greater density of them in the same way that a city might be saturated with invisible electromagnetic waves. In other localities the electromagnetic waves are still around, although their activity is greatly reduced. It's worth repeating that usually we're aware of the areas where we feel we lack rank and unaware of the areas where we're full of it. We can't hide our rank because, unwittingly, we announce it all of the time. Others pick up on it through our communication style and the 'signals' we emit, either with intention or not. Sometimes our signalling of either high or low rank is strong, other times less so. Many times the signals are subtle and discreet, which makes them hard to grasp hold of, slippery to change and difficult to defend against if they're being directed at us personally. Whoever 'receives' the rank signals we generate will then modify this information according to visual and other details they perceive about us. They will take into account our accent, for instance, appearance, gender, age or ethnicity and, very quickly, assess relative rank and what this translates to in terms of power. All of us are adept at doing this, even if we have no conscious awareness that this is the case. We need a lot of commitment, patience and humility to peel back and reveal our own rank, and then to weigh how we use it. Differences of rank and power can't be eliminated through goodwill alone. Take a look at this list of some low-rank signals and see if you can get a feel for what I mean here:

- deferential eye contact (in Western cultures)
- stumbling over words
- high levels of bodily discomfort such as feeling hot, or having sticky palms
- remaining silent when you want to speak
- 'putting on' a show of confidence
- taking up little physical space
- agreeing with every suggestion
- asking for permission rather than being assertive
- complying with actions you disagree with.

Conversely, high-rank signals may look like this:

- taking up 'air-time' at a meeting or event
- denying the feelings or lived experience of another person
- minimising the grievances of others
- victim blaming (e.g. 'I overcame adversity, so you do the same')
- taking up physical space
- playing by different rules to those the majority have to follow (e.g. arriving late and not apologising)
- making assumptions and not checking them out
- using exclusive language, either deliberately or with no awareness
- intentionally mis-gendering someone
- mocking, 'teasing' or using sarcasm as standard communication.

Remember, power, privilege and rank is a language with its own grammar and syntax. When we learn this language, we can both interpret what's being 'said' to us at any given moment and then choose our response.

In the service of our kids

I hope you're able to see that discussing power in this way isn't an intellectual exercise that's disconnected from your child's safety and well-being. When we own our rank as parents and caregivers, and cultivate a good working knowledge of how power is exercised, we're positioning ourselves as agents of change in the lives of our children. Such effort is the core emotional, psychological and, yes, political, work of changing rampant gender prejudice and discrimination that put all children at risk. If we, as parents and caregivers to gender-expansive kids, don't do this work, who will? Fundamentally, our perceptions, privilege and resulting rank and entitlement will either promote the ongoing policing of gender or puncture it. There is no middle ground.

Language, labelling and 'laughing things off...'

We live in a world that's permeated by stories. Stories about how we, as human beings, should live and relate to everything that's around us, including the Earth and all its other inhabitants. The stories spell out to us what's right or wrong, who's good or bad, what will bring happiness to us or not, what we can and can't do, who we should and shouldn't be. Such cultural narratives are embedded everywhere, so these stories are active in our minds and shape how we think, feel and act. When a lot of people hold onto a particular story, it takes root culturally as consensus reality. It then becomes accepted as a 'truth', and its origins rarely get questioned.

In the early part of the 20th century, when World War I commenced, the dominant story for men was of patriotism, duty and heroism. Hence, when a soldier fled the frontline and was captured and returned to his battalion, he was, tragically, shot for cowardice. Now we would call the soldier's unremitting terror 'post-traumatic stress disorder'. Throughout the same century and into this one, the dominant story has been that education and intelligence equate to the same thing. Hence, thousands upon thousands of children who struggled to read were once stigmatised as being 'stupid'. Now we call these bright young people 'dyslexic'. Gangs who routinely beat up gay men when I was a teenager, called their ugly sport 'queer bashing'.[4] Now we call this what it is: 'homophobia'. I'm hoping you'll recognise in such examples that cultural stories are always in a process of change, and language is a senior midwife in this. So, too, it is with gender. Like any birth, things do not always progress easily. The old story, which may well have been a radical one of its time, becomes outdated. If we hold onto it, it will obstruct the cultural birth canal and impede the birth of the new story – the one that's being called for now in these times. Make no mistake about it, language has magical properties. When we name something, we bring it alive. That's why it's so critical that we, as allies, become active participants in the gender stories we live by, and not merely passive recipients of them.

Words are not value-free, and neither are they all benign. They can heal and they can harm, support or sting, include or exclude. They affect us psychologically, emotionally, spiritually and physically. I confess that I've approached the writing of this entire chapter with some trepidation. I'm not a linguistic scholar or a philosopher. I am a writer though and I regard language with the same awe as I do anything else that's truly mysterious. As allies we need to understand

---

4   The word 'queer' was reclaimed in the 1980s by scholars and activists to establish community, and make explicit an identity that was distinct from gay identity.

why it occupies such a pivotal role in protecting our children and treating them fairly. And we need to be able to explain this to other people. Anyone who's serious about supporting us will take the time to listen.

Language as a culture-keeper

Cultural stories are created, protected and held in place by the way we use language. The Gender Matrix and other comparable systems that coerce conformity depend, absolutely, on its uncritical use. They depend on language either becoming so normalised that an implicit message goes unheard, or so monopolised that explicit messages go unchallenged. I've heard it said that paying close attention to words is creating a problem where one didn't exist before. I've also heard it said that interrogating language is 'political correctness gone mad'. If people only engage with this issue at a 'head' level and not a 'heart' one, then they will find themselves taken hostage by political correctness, it's true. Conformity is the sallow cousin of conviction. When you observe the hostages, you'll see that they 'watch' what they say, though their actions will be rigid and their attitude self-conscious. In contrast, aspiring to include people on the basis of kindness, dignity and a genuine desire to include them, isn't something I feel offended by. Anyone who claims their values include fairness and respect for others shouldn't need convincing about the role of language in this. Language is used to both draw the line and to bring people in line. And the way gender rules are still enforced is a perfect example of this.

Typically, men who are too emotionally expressive, or deemed to not be aggressive enough, are targets of the culture-keepers. Similarly, women who take up 'unfeminine' job roles, or are judged to be too independent of men, may become targeted. In these specific cases and more generally, when aggression is intended, language is a weapon. The man or boy is accused of either being 'like a girl' or gay. Or the sexual reputation of his female partner, his sister or his mother is brought into question. The purpose of this behaviour is to humiliate the man by branding him effeminate and not 'man enough' to control 'his' women. This convicts him of not being a, 'real man'. Similarly, the most common insult a woman or girl is subject to still revolves around some sort of sexual slur, implying she's either frigid, promiscuous or lesbian. All of these contravene heterosexist male standards for women. I wish I could report that this was an outdated story that has zero relevance to us. Sadly, this isn't the case.

According to *The School Report*,[5] extensive research undertaken by the LGBT charity, Stonewall, 98 per cent of gay pupils and 95 per cent of teachers hear 'that's so gay' or 'you're so gay' at school, while insults such as 'poof', 'dyke' and 'lezza' are regularly used to 'tease', demean, or regulate peer behaviour. What scares me most about statistics such as these is how acceptable this language has been allowed to become. It isn't 'just kids' being mean to each other, which absolves adults and institutions from having to take any responsibility. The prevalence of language such as this could not have taken root unless the context permitted it. As one young trans teen conveyed to me about her time in secondary school, 'I was a deer being mercilessly hunted down by my peers. I was victimised lesson after lesson and teachers, shamelessly, looked away.' Indeed, pupils reported that only 10 per cent of teachers challenge homophobic language every time they hear it, and three in five LGBT pupils reported that teachers don't intervene when they witness homophobic bullying. Only 50 per cent of pupils reported that their schools explicitly stated homophobic bullying was wrong, and this figure was lower for faith schools, at 37 per cent. With more than half the respondents experiencing bullying such as this, small wonder that 44 per cent of them skip school. I'm surprised this statistic is not higher. As the mother of

---

5   Guasp, A. and Statham, H. (2015) *The School Report (2012)*. Stonewall and the University of Cambridge Centre for Family Research. Available at www.stonewall. org.uk/resources/school-report-2012, accessed on 14 July 2017.

Eva, the young trans woman whose school so seriously betrayed their duty to her, told me:

> Taking a child to an unsafe place every day, and trying to encourage them to get an education when they're spending all their energy trying to cope with what's being said to them, and done to them, was a horrifying experience. She was exhausted with the bullying. The school put all the responsibility on her. I did feel it was a real attempt, the way it was dragged out, it was a real attempt to exhaust us both.

The research is clear. In schools where homophobic language is the norm, bullying is nearly double compared to schools that have sought to eliminate it. This finding makes something else absolutely explicit: it damns the leadership of any school where this culture has been allowed to become the norm.

Derogatory terms to do with gender and sexuality are littered throughout the English language. You know some of them. I know some of them. And there are a thousand more neither of us know. When it becomes acceptable to direct these missiles at gender non-conforming kids on the basis of their difference, something is terribly wrong. An unspoken assumption is in operation that gives others permission to do so. That assumption is that people have the right to be insensitive towards our children and, at worst, to attack them. Words can hurt even if their use is convincingly justified; even if there's no conscious intent to harm. Words can pierce our children's hearts as effectively as any missile. And sometimes the hearts of children haemorrhage. Language has the power to serve or to destroy, depending on how it's used and what it's trying to achieve. Sexism, cisgenderism, homophobia and transphobia are a quartet of cultural bullies with interlocked arms. They work as a gang and control the same turf. They speak the same language, only with different dialects. All of them are culture-keepers. They're invested in an old story and untouched by how much suffering it causes. When we undermine one of them, we undermine all of them. We should make it our business to do so as often as possible.

Language that labels

Labelling occurs when a person becomes categorised across society, based on a stereotype about the group they belong to. A stereotype is an oversimplified or generalised idea about a group of people, often held by members of a different group. It might be positive, such as 'all elderly people are trustworthy', or negative, such as 'all people on welfare benefits don't want to work'. Either way, it will be based on limited knowledge and will discount any individual features belonging to people within the stereotyped group. Stereotypes aren't, of themselves, wrong. As a species, we're bombarded at an incredible speed with information and stimuli. Our brains are designed to make quick judgements, to categorise and ascertain if there's any threat or benefit in what we're perceiving. Stereotypes help us to make 'quick sense' of the world and this gives us a measure of control. They create 'short-cuts' in our mental processes so we don't get exhausted filtering everything in detail. Stereotypes only become destructive when they underscore prejudice and justify discrimination.

Because our psychology is hardwired to organise information via mental short-cuts, it's unrealistic to imagine that we can avoid stereotyping others. What we can do is train ourselves to notice when our own feeling, thinking and behaviour is being influenced by stereotypes and learn to identify when, how and why we might label others because of this. For instance, a short while ago I was eating in a 'nice' restaurant in town. It was busy with early evening guests who, like me, were taking advantage of a special offer. My table was near the reception desk and I was enjoying my meal and 'people watching', which is one of my favourite things to do. At one point an Indian man, wearing the customary turban of the Sikh faith, approached the empty reception area and hovered there until the head waiter arrived. A short conversation ensued and then, to my surprise, the man was shown to a table. In this instance I was able to notice my response, surprise, and it alerted me to the fact that I had been stereotyping this person. I'd assumed he was a taxi-driver and not someone, like me, who was a patron of the restaurant. In this circumstance, the stereotype I'd generated didn't cause any harm and, especially so, because I recognised it for what it was. Unhappily, that cannot be said when we look at the bigger picture. Stereotypes are used to exacerbate fear, create divisions, support mainstream interests and, very often, to profit a powerful minority.

Tabloid newspapers exemplify the relationship between stereotyping and negative labelling: *every* Muslim is a terrorist, *every* person with mental health challenges is a 'psycho', *every* espoused feminist is a 'man-hater', *every* transgender student is a threat to cis-safety. For myself, I find such manipulation of language inexcusable because it has no concern for the damage it leaves in its wake.[6] We must be mindful of what we absorb, as well as what we express. Gandhi said it well: 'I will not let anyone walk through my mind with their dirty feet.'

Negative labels, be they gross and extreme, or subtle and seductive, attribute a value judgement that can be almost impossible to defend oneself fully against. Often they will twist around a person's sense of self as shame. Shame grows roots when such labels go unnoticed, ignored, encouraged or, worse still, applauded. In such a circumstance, a label can brand itself like a third-degree burn on a person's psyche, which left untended can lead to dire consequences.

A label lasts when a person absorbs it as a truth about themselves. In other words, they come to believe the myths and misinformation that's been foisted onto them by society at large. This may happen because a foundation of toxic shame has been laid down in them, or

6   A coroner ruled in 2013 that Lucy Meadows, a primary school teacher in the United Kingdom who was also a transgender woman, killed herself after being hounded by the media. He closed the inquest on her death with this comment to the reporters who were present: 'And to you the press, I say shame, shame on all of you.'

because they've been repeatedly subject to exploitation, anger or abuse from other people. Children and young people in the care system are a high-risk group in these circumstances. When a label becomes owned, it's called 'internalised oppression'. Internalised oppression is a canker that becomes self-harm. It's this that drives many people to hurt themselves, not necessarily any difference they carry, as is often assumed. That's why labelling is such an important issue for us, as allies, to understand. As I search around in my mind for an example to offer you, again, I don't need to look any further than my own conduct. For instance, in my city, typically, a homeless person will sit on a flattened-out piece of cardboard, with an empty paper cup in front of them on the pavement. On some occasions, usually when I'm feeling frazzled or in a hurry, I'll purposely widen the physical distance between myself and the person as I approach them, or pick up my speed and avoid all eye contact. At times like these, to my regret now, I'm responding to the label 'homeless' and not to a human being whose experience is taking place in a social context. I'm ignoring the lack of affordable housing where I live, the sky-high rents that private landlords often dictate, or the fact that, without an address, it's impossible to find employment. I'm disregarding the domestic violence, bereavement and sexual abuse that often precede homelessness. The point is, depending on my own levels of awareness at the time, I either collude with labelling, or I resist it. When it's the former, I'm perpetuating a situation that underscores prejudice and discrimination, irrespective of how the person became destitute. On the occasions when I do stop and talk, ask the person their name, give them money or buy them a sandwich, I not only connect to their humanity, I re-connect to my own.

Our child's gender journey is happening both within language and within the wider context of society, where many factions label it as 'wrong' in some way. The more familiar we are with how this prejudice gets acted out, the more able we become to confront it, and to equip our children to do so too. Jude has been fearless in teaching Ruby about this:

I've been very honest with Ruby about the world and about prejudice and the fact that there are lots of people in the world who don't understand difference – any kind difference. It might be the colour of someone's skin, it might be that they're transgender, it might be that they don't want to be a gender. We've been very clear with Ruby that there are people in the world who are prejudiced. And we've explained what prejudice is, that it's wrong, not right, whether it's about ourselves or other people. I've said we should defend other people, and we should expect to be defended.

Dialogues such as this one can't prevent any child from being the target of prejudice, but they will protect a child from being drip-fed toxic shame. Know this: the gender tide is turning. We can safeguard the worth of our children and honour their difference. It's never too late to confront the labelling our kids are subject to, and it's never too early to start.

Labels that evade us

We live in a society that's saturated with labels. If the label doesn't apply to us, then we frequently won't register it, usually because we don't *feel* it personally. When this is the case, which means often, we must apprentice ourselves to hearing when language is being used against, not on behalf of, someone else. And this isn't possible to do without listening well. Many of us are poor at listening. We have a running dialogue going on in our heads as we measure what we hear against our assumptions and judgements. If what we hear doesn't fit our personal 'map of the world', then we simply discount it, as though that's the end of the matter. These habits and behaviours sabotage our development as compassionate human beings.

As allies, we must learn to listen at depth and allow ourselves to feel our response to it. This is essential. So often in these situations we counter our gut feeling with a rational thought, such as 'I'm sure they didn't mean it', or an illogical one, such as 'they probably didn't notice' (referring to the person being labelled). When we cancel out our true feeling like this, we're teaching ourselves to become numb. In time, this creates a situation where we've inadvertently opted for willing ignorance and we're participating in prejudice.

When I was a social worker, the professional acronym for 'Looked after Children'[7] was LAC. We'd have LAC reviews, LAC sessions in school, LAC training and LAC family support meetings. It was a student social worker who brought my attention to the labelling implicit in this acronym. Although I had used it daily, I never 'heard' what she did as a newcomer to our organisation. Not only did it reinforce the social stigma children in care experienced, it reinforced their innumerable losses too. LAC: Lacking a 'normal' family life, lacking stability in school, lacking contact with people they loved, lacking reputation in the community, lacking influence over what might happen to them. No child, young person or family member I ever worked with mentioned the prolific use of this term. Perhaps they never 'heard' it either? Perhaps it matched their internal reality? Perhaps the rank I had as a social work professional completely dwarfed theirs in this context? I can only hazard a guess.

I respected the young student for challenging the language we were habitually using. It was a brave move in a group setting where she had little status. Challenges always present us with a series of choices and this one presented me, as a manager, with several. The first choice I made was to listen to the student and not become defensive or use my rank to 'close her down'. My second choice was to listen to myself for a corresponding echo of truth, or not, in what she had to say. And my third choice was to decide on any action I wanted to take in response to this process. Ultimately, the experience led to changes within my work environment and changes within myself. Since then, I've co-facilitated training with a number of care-experienced

---

7   This term is still current and widespread within the United Kingdom.

young people. It hasn't been lost on me that, in this setting, when the power balance between us is consciously addressed, almost all of them expressed a dislike for this term. In their eyes, when someone's aware enough to recognise the mixed message in it, what they see is respect and empathy at work, not political correctness.

There's a principle here that can be carried across to other targeted differences. When we have the luxury of engaging in debates about labelling from a purely theoretical perspective, we must be careful. In essence, we can afford to approach the matter from a cool, detached perspective because we don't have anything to lose. That's a privilege.

Language and humour – 'laughing things off...'

The expression, 'I was only joking' is normally the first defence of a person who's been challenged about their humour. When this happens, we always have two choices: we can do our best to receive the feedback graciously and reflect on it, or we can become brittle and insist the fault lies with the other person – usually, because we judge them to be 'over-sensitive', expecting special treatment or not capable of 'taking a joke'. Does any of this sound familiar to you? Notice here that I'm not focusing on the aggrieved person 'taking offence'. Too often, this is another mechanism for drawing attention away from the person who's made the joke, and back onto the person who's objected to it. For me, it's much more useful to consider impact. At the level of impact, I have to consider whether I'm responsible for hurting someone's feelings, or not. My culpability can't seamlessly disappear behind well-honed defences such as 'You've got a chip on your shoulder.'

Salt, or chilli, or vinegar will leave a foul taste in our mouth if there's too much of it in any dish. When humour is used to undermine or exclude someone, it can have the same effect on us. We invariably *know* when someone has 'gone too far'. We either pretend that we don't realise and remain silent (which, in group dynamic terms, is called 'colluding'), or we intervene. This might range from a quick aside to a direct challenge, depending on the circumstances and the people involved. There isn't one way to do this, except courageously and with integrity. It helps, enormously, if we can add skilfully. Ideally we're looking for a win–win situation over a stand-off, or a stand-down that isn't sincere. I want to be clear here: I'm not making any sort of case for eliminating humour from our interactions. I'm British. I've been born and bred into the sort of self-deprecating and droll humour Brits are known for. I can banter and retort with the best of them. What I'm saying is specific: when humour is combined with group membership, power and relative rank, it can become a recipe for absolute misery.

I once had a friend who was part of a 'macho' profession. He was a gregarious man, with a quick wit and generous attitude. He did well in work and was offered a promotion in another part of the country. After due consideration, he accepted the opportunity, left my area and we lost contact. Years later we connected again and, eventually, he told me what had happened after he'd started his new job. Initially he did well and accrued merit, but soon someone in his new team took an intense dislike to him for no reason he could fathom. It started as a 'bit of fun' and, in the beginning, my friend tried to go along with it as much as he could. He wanted to fit in, make new buddies and bring the best of himself to the role he was in. But things didn't improve. The banter in the group took on a sharper edge and gradually colleagues from across the team began to withdraw from him. If, on occasions anyone expressed sympathy for him, they always did so privately and never in front of the other team members. Soon my friend found himself isolated and targeted by people he once thought he might look to for support. This went on for two years. Towards the end of this time, feeling shamed by his situation and daily tormented, he began running as a way to manage his stress levels. The bullying intensified and soon he found himself crying as he ran to work and crying as he ran home. Not long after, he had a complete breakdown. Casual observers might have observed 'banter' that sometimes 'crossed the line' and one person in a group being the butt of all the jokes. They may have wondered why my friend was never included in social events or why he always ate his lunch alone. The observers might even have registered that something was 'off' in some way but put that thought to one side. Or considered that perhaps my friend was too reserved, or even aloof. They might even have blamed him for not 'standing up for himself'. But the observers' partial views, based on fleeting evidence, snapshot opinions and self-interest, meant my friend, in real terms, was abandoned to the pack.

If an adult can suffer in such a shocking and sustained way, how much more vulnerable are children? We should offer absolutely no leeway to any adult who persists in 'teasing', making a joke of, or otherwise humiliating our child when we've asked them to stop. It doesn't matter if people accuse us of being 'politically correct', 'over-the-top', or 'defensive'. What matters is that we are taking a position we can respect ourselves for. This is child-inclusive parenting that always takes account of power, privilege and rank. It will test you. I know because it tests me almost every time a situation demands it. But what matters more to me than my discomfort, is that I square up to each situation and do my best. As an ally, do I have any other choice?

CHAPTER 7

LABELS THAT HELP OR HINDER OUR CHILDREN

Ruby is a girl child who is happy. She rarely references this as exceptional and when she does, at least for now, it's in positive terms. Ruby continues to surprise us. A few months ago her dad recounted to me a conversation he'd witnessed between Ruby and her younger sister, Rosa. Rosa had referred to her older sister as her brother. At this point Ruby gently intervened and said, 'I'm not your brother, Rosa. I used to be but I'm not now. I'm transgender, so that means I'm your sister.' My son-in-law was completely taken aback. As a family our concern has always been to allow Ruby her experience, rather than to name it in any way for her. Once again, she took the next step. When her dad asked her later about where she'd heard this term, she told him brightly that she'd read it in her 'Jazz book'[1] and had realised then that it described how she felt. I'm glad that Ruby has found the word that best reflects her sense of who she is at the moment. And I'm open to the possibility that this may change, or not, as Ruby leaves childhood behind and enters early adolescence.

The issue of labelling Ruby's behaviour was 'live' from the beginning of her gender journey. Initially my response was defensive when people queried if we'd sought a diagnosis for it. *'Why would*

---

1   Herthel, J. (2015) *I Am Jazz*. New York, NY: Dial Books. This book had been in the house for some time, but it was only when Ruby learnt to read for herself that she expressed any real interest in it.

we do that?' I'd reply. *'You only need a diagnosis if you think there's a problem.'* My defensiveness gradually gave way to a softer attitude as I gained a foothold on this new territory. That was a curve in the road it was important for me to find my way around. This all seems quite a long time ago now. Now Ruby is…just Ruby. In the way that any of my other precious grandchildren simply are who they are to me. But, unlike her sister and her cousins, Ruby is both unravelling and following a particular Golden Thread. It's likely that the closer she gets to puberty the more knots she may discover in it. My faith in her to free them up for herself remains strong. I have concerns that lie elsewhere. A diagnostic label may be non-negotiable in the not-too-distant future to ensure Ruby's needs are met. And there is a risk, as many of you will know, that the Golden Thread will become tangled in the hands of other people if they do not take sufficient care.

There have been decades of controversy surrounding the professional classification of gender variance in children. If you believe, as I do, in a gender-affirmative model of care, that is, a model that accepts variations of gender as a natural aspect of being human, then progress has been made. As Dr Ehrensaft makes clear:

> In the gender affirmative model…[that] children are the experts of their own gender self, and, at most, we adults are their translators – striving to understand what they are telling us about their gender in words, actions, feelings, thoughts and relationships.[2]

Presently, the current term 'Gender identity disorder of childhood', as cited in the *ICD-10*,[3] is under revision by the World Health Organization (WHO). Weight appears to be leaning towards the

---

2   Ehrensaft, D. (2016) *The Gender Creative Child: Pathways for Nurturing and Supporting Children Who Live Outside Gender Boxes.* New York, NY: The Experiment, LLC, p.16.

3   The *International Classification of Diseases (ICD)* (1990) is used by healthcare providers and researchers.

new diagnostic label Gender Incongruity in Childhood (GIC). The WHO working party believe, though not unanimously, that this term balances the need for change with the need for caution, until a sufficient body of research dictates otherwise. Their belief is that this term will depathologise gender variance, as they propose to move the reformulated category out of the *ICD*'s mental disorder chapter and into another 'medical' part of the classification. Amongst other things, they are confident GIC will safeguard access to care for children and young people in an evolving, mixed provision landscape. Opponents of the term remain unconvinced. They contend that in many cultures gender diversity is so organic it barely creates a flicker of interest. Significantly, they argue, childhood gender variance doesn't require any medical interventions such as hormone therapy or surgical procedures, so why frame the experience of children as a dis-ease in some way? If a child is distressed by their difference, which is often a result of being victimised because of it, support can be accessed under the same diagnosis as any child with clinical depression or anxiety. Why persist in pathologising gender, they ask, when the history of pathologising sexuality grimaces back at us?

The debate is intense and involves a multitude of stakeholders, across many disciplines, sometimes with competing agendas. As allies and child-inclusive parents and caregivers, it's our right to occupy this territory too. Indeed, to occupy the centre of it. By this I don't mean to suggest that we must be fully informed about, or comprehend every detail of this debate. My personal view is that no one individual is in a position to do this. I do mean, however, that without our voices, the debate is utterly impoverished. Our position in the lives of our gender-expansive children means that we hold a piece of the truth that no-one else can. Andrew Solomon, in his deeply compassionate book *Far from the Tree* casts a far-ranging net over this complex territory. Ultimately he comes down on one side of it:

> How we name something determined how we perceive it... As long as GID is classified as a mental illness, professionals will try to cure it, and parents will refuse to accept it. It is time to focus on the child rather than on the label.[4]

You and I and our kids, be they birth children, grandchildren, step-children, nieces, nephews or foster-children, are implicated in this discourse, willingly or not. The terms we integrate into language eventually take concrete form in a person's life, one way or another. There's a mainline between diagnostic terms, supply and outcomes, and gate-keepers at each of the doorways. Who a professional perceives our child to be, disordered or well, can either unlock, or lock up the resources our child may need. Again, as parents and caregivers, we're tasked with the sobering duty of making sense of all this, while making decisions that, potentially, will shape our children's lives forever. Dr Ehrensaft offers this advice to all of us:

> I have had the good fortune of working with the most wonderful of paediatricians who will make every effort to ensure that their gender non-conforming and transgender young patients get the care and attention they need to grow up healthy. I would encourage the parents of any gender non-conforming child to search high and low for just such a doctor, which sometimes means having to leave the paediatrician that has up until then served all the children in the family.[5]

This search may be frustrating and demoralising. It may even be frightening if medics use their power and rank to undermine, or

---

4   Solomon, A. (2014) *Far from the Tree: Parents, Children and the Search for Identity*. London: Penguin Random House, p.608.

5   Ehrensaft, D. (2016) *The Gender Creative Child: Pathways for Nurturing and Supporting Children Who Live Outside Gender Boxes*. New York, NY: The Experiment, LLC, p.187.

intimidate, parents and caregivers. Nevertheless, we must still go door-to-door following leads and recommendations. Eventually, we'll find the professionals who are worthy of our child's care, and the trust we're prepared to place in them.

This is the journey Gillian and Andrew, an articulate middle-class couple, undertook on behalf of their young trans son, Charlie. For months their boy had been retreating into feelings of hopelessness as he struggled, and failed, to meet the 'criteria' clinicians were insisting he conform to. As the couple tried, and failed, to work in collaboration with the team who were dealing with Charlie they repeatedly met with the behaviours I've described above. As Charlie became more and more reclusive, the worries Gillian and Andrew already had started to escalate significantly. Their search began. In the end, the family had to travel some distance to find practitioners they could depend on. I asked Gillian how she knew the doctor they found could be trusted, after everything the family had been through. She closed her eyes for a moment and her face relaxed as she opened them. This is what she said:

> What was striking is that from the outset, it was so much more than a standard 'therapeutic relationship'. It had an openness to it that elicited the sort of respect and trust that we probably experience more commonly with close family and friends. When all our tears fell, because we'd reached this safe place, the doctor's response was a demonstration of human compassion, genuine care and reassurance: 'It's okay, I understand. I'm listening to everything you tell me and we're going to work out the best plan for you and make it happen.' The sheer relief of finding someone who could listen, but actually hear, was immense. Later on Charlie wrote to the consultant, he said, 'Thank you for giving me a future.' My son had a future so everything we had to do was worth it.

The right to self-definition

Who we identify as cuts to the core of being human. The right to self-define is the right to choose or accept labels that match our internal reality. Some of the contemporary ways to express this may be new, but the drive to name our own experience is not. Throughout history until the present day, if the mainstream disputes an identity, then it will have to be fought for in order to endure. When we name something, it bequeaths life; if we refuse to, it remains invisible. Language is a form of resistance. When we speak, we demand visibility. That's why the native language of subjugated peoples must always be erased. That's why poets get jailed alongside politicians, journalists disappear as well as generals, and authors perish next to ambassadors. That's why, for non-mainstream groups in particular, the right to define their own story is essential to their survival. As Audre Lorde shared with us of her own experience, 'If I didn't define myself for myself, I would be crunched into other people's fantasies of me and eaten alive.'[6]

My daughter, Jude, has stepped into the eye of this particular storm, both in how she stands up for Ruby's right to define herself, and in how she teaches Ruby to do the same:

> I remember saying to Ruby, 'When people say to you that you shouldn't be wearing a dress, do you think they're right or wrong?' And she said, 'They're wrong', and I said, 'They *are* wrong. They're absolutely wrong because you're a girl and you should be wearing a dress.' That was really important to me to say. Normally I would say to a child, 'Well, you know, you've got to respect everybody's opinions' and things like that, but with this,

---

6   Lorde, A. (1982) 'Learning from the 60s.' Presentation during Malcolm X weekend at Harvard University, February 1982. Available at www.blackpast.org/1982-audre-lorde-learning-60s, accessed on 14 July 2017.

I thought it was really important for Ruby to know that this was absolutely wrong, that it's a violation of her human rights. I said to her, 'Now you've told us that you're a girl, we understand that, but what we need to think about is what we're going to say to those people who don't. Most people might say it's fabulous, and you look brilliant in your girl's school uniform, but some might not.' I asked her, 'Has anybody ever said anything about it to you?' She said, 'Yes, so and so. He always says I should be wearing trousers.' I said, 'What do you say to him?' She said, 'I don't say anything, I just ignore him.' I remember sitting on the bed and saying, 'Ruby, okay, this is what we're going to do: we're going to talk about how we hold our body, where we hold our head, and what we can say in response to people who behave like this.' It made me feel empowered, as a parent, to know that I'd given my child the resources to deal with those kinds of challenges.

The theoretical field of language and gender is still very young and, what's more, it's extremely fast-moving. The context our children find themselves in is light years away from their grandparents', if not their parents' early lives. We live in an age of super-diversity. According to research from the Institute of Public Policy Research in the United Kingdom, 'Britain is not only more diverse than ever before but that diversity itself is growing more diverse. Today, identities are more complex and fluid than they used to be, reflecting shifting interests and alliances.'[7] Plainly put, today's youth don't buy into the old 'tick-box' approach of identifying oneself as this or that. First, they appreciate the infinite variety within any one category such as 'Asian' or 'Heterosexual', and, secondly, they declare multiple identities that

7   Fanshawe, S. and Sriskandarajah, D. (2010) 'You can't put me in a box: Super-diversity and the end of identity politics in Britain.' Institute for Public Policy Research (IPPR). Available at www.ippr.org/publications/you-cant-put-me-in-a-box-super-diversity-and-the-end-of-identity politics-in-britain, accessed on 14 July 2017.

overlap. Modern technology is the magic carpet that has transported them to this destination over the last 15 years. Children and young people are natives of this brave new world, while the rest of us are travellers and tourists. When we factor in the primacy of social media in the lives of our youth, we're looking at a moving train. To illustrate my point, Facebook now has 53 gender categories to choose from. When I discovered this, a part of me immediately piped up with 'Oh my goodness, that's ridiculous.' But I would say that, wouldn't I? I'm cisgender, so I've never had to habitually identify myself as someone I'm not. Or deal with the consequences of that over a lifetime. The gender story I've lived by, has for the most part, served me well. My reactivity reminds me again that so often our first response is to dismiss something we don't understand. Carl Jung's wise words chastise my sloppy self-talk: 'Thinking is difficult. That's why people judge.'[8]

Earlier this year I attended a conference called 'Moving beyond the Binaries of Sex and Gender' at the University of Leeds, England. I was somewhat apprehensive beforehand as I'd never been in an environment where, as a cisgender woman, it was likely I'd be outnumbered. When I arrived, for the first time in my life, someone asked me what my preferred pronouns were. She requested that I write them next to my name on the sticky label she handed to me. As I did so, then looked around at everyone else who was doing the same, I liked the fact that there were no pre-printed badges classifying the people around me. Instead, my eyes had to search out each delegate's label, written in wavy or even script, in different coloured inks. It was a good beginning to my day. The international panel of speakers were insightful and thought-provoking, and the spoken-word poetry and music engaged my brain, imagination and heart. And still the thing that affected me the most was writing my own pronouns and addressing others by theirs. I was disoriented

8   Attributed to Carl Jung.

when I did this, afraid I'd 'get it wrong' and quite self-conscious for a lot of the time. As the afternoon drew to a close, I felt humbled, primarily because this experience mirrored back to me something I take entirely for granted. Several times that day I had imagined how it might be to experience things differently. If, for instance, someone used language to deliberately alienate me; or if my pronouns, instead of being respected, were distorted or converted into material for ridicule. My attendance at the conference gave me the opportunity to afford others the same respect that I, as someone cisgender, enjoy every day. And I also found it liberating. In acknowledging, through language, the various identities present, I left the gentle monotony of my own conformity and discovered, outside of it, a garden of gender diversity.

Yet language still continues to confound us, because when we name anything, it's only ever in comparison to something else. Even when we intend and want to be inclusive, acronyms are defined by who they don't include, as much as who they do. As Jaimee Garbacik states so well in *Gender and Sexuality for Beginners*, 'We keep leaving people behind in favour of the simplest, most easily digested vision of an empowered future.'[9] Her solution, regrettably, is a rare one: 'The more adults trust and listen to young people, the more visibility and access they attain, the better we will all become at articulating how labels are barriers.'[10] We must hope that as our awareness grows, terminology will evolve with it. Meanwhile, the 53 gender categories that Facebook offers is a beginning. They equate to abundance, when before there was only scarcity; recognition when before there was erasure; and community over isolation. Who am I to judge this as ridiculous? Someone with privilege, who just about has a handle on some of it, for some of the time.

---

9   Garbacik, J. (2013) *Gender and Sexuality for Beginners*. Danbury, CT: For Beginners LLC, p.3.
10 Garbacik, J. (2013) *Gender and Sexuality for Beginners*. Danbury, CT: For Beginners LLC, p.4.

CHAPTER 8

APPROACHING THE MATRIX

Turning inwards

We have been scaling the walls of the Gender Matrix together. Getting a feel for the bricks and mortar, the structures and scaffolding that keeps it standing. We know by now, if we didn't before, that the Gender Matrix is a force to be reckoned with. On a micro level it influences our thoughts, attitudes, expectations and behaviour, while on a macro scale it's the cornerstone of culture across the globe. It's everywhere, all of the time, invisible and formidable. It rewards us with benefits and bonuses when we conform to it, and punishes us with stigma and deprivation when we don't. This is the circumstance our children have been born into.

The Matrix is founded on a 'one size fits all' ideology that's presented as 'common sense'. This gives it an air of respectability and authority, as though any other reality is merely the figment of a child's imagination or a young person 'acting out'. It treats these experiences as fictitious, as though the organisation of gender, as we know it, isn't. As we've gone further into the recesses of the Matrix, we've discovered some shocking things: erased histories, forgotten graves, rules written in blood and rocks to stone dissenters with. This is not a place of welcome.

Determining to dismantle the Matrix inside of yourself is a momentous decision. In effect, you're saying to yourself and to the world that this structure has been a safe and secure dimension of my homeland and I am leaving because now I understand that some people are held here against their will. They're coerced into conforming and made to be wrong if they don't. Even little ones are not always safe here. Some are taught that the Golden Thread in their small warm hand is only a filthy bit of yarn tying them to a lie.

If you're to love your child unconditionally and promote their well-being exhaustively, then time is of the essence. This half of the book is a call to action. Its starting point is exactly where you are now, which is the perfect place to begin. First, we'll look at four internal domains that you, exclusively, are the gate-keeper of: self-knowledge, self-awareness, self-esteem and self-forgiveness. I think of these four domains as the 'Four Ss', the foundational cornerstones on which to construct your own personal matrix. The interacting relationship between them all will provide you with the strength, stability and flexibility you need to succeed in this endeavour. Each one is substantial in itself, and together they create more than the sum of their parts. As you lay them in place, alongside the Four Keys – listening, imagination, empathy and courage – you've empowered yourself to demolish the Matrix. And, by association, to fully accept and protect the gender-expansive child you love and are responsible for. Know that this is ground you can stand on. From here you can dismantle the Matrix in your psyche, piece by piece.

Self-knowledge: Why is it important to you as an ally?

Self-knowledge leads to agency

Self-knowledge, in my view, is one of the greatest assets we have as allies to our gender-expansive kids. It enables us, over time, to discern the mark of the Matrix in our minds. To have knowledge about ourselves – why we think and behave as we do, what values matter to us, what our shortcomings are, what we're prepared to stand for or against, what we resist and what we welcome – creates meaning for us. And human beings are meaning-making creatures. Self-knowledge also creates the possibility of an empowered life. This is because substantial self-knowledge leads to what developmental psychologists refer to as 'agency': the capacity to influence what happens to us. Agency arises out of taking responsibility for our lives and exercising choice to improve it. It means learning to tell ourselves the truth. This might translate into a concerted effort to curb our social drinking, or to arrange a meeting with our bank manager, or to disclose to our partner feelings we haven't shared with them before. Agency means being proactive in your own life.

Children have very little true agency. Their reality is frequently denied and they often suffer significantly as a result of their low rank. This renders them highly vulnerable, and dependent, on the adults around them – sometimes with tragic consequences. We do well to imaginatively put ourselves in the shoes of children as often as possible. So a child-inclusive parent or caregiver who has a strong degree of agency, undoubtedly, is a force to be reckoned with as an empowered ally. In a child's mind, they are a giant – a giant they can shelter behind and depend on to shield and protect them. This is a bulletproof protective factor in the psyche of any child.

Self-knowledge leads to accomplished parenting

Our primary goal as a loving parent is to facilitate a sturdy, embodied identity in our child. Such an identity is built on the experience of a child feeling cherished through unconditional love, which includes freedom within appropriate limits. It also includes the necessity to repeatedly let our children 'go' as they develop and mature. Inevitably, our own identity journey will influence our child's. Making a study of how is a wise thing to do. Yoking together our family history, relationships, events and circumstances that have made up our own life, and how we've responded to them both consciously and unconsciously, educates us at a deep level. We recognise that the beliefs, habits, behaviours, characteristics and personality traits we possess are not random. They have a genesis in our life story, even though it's usually an impossible task to locate where single-handedly. This self-knowledge can be used twice: first, to enhance our agency as individuals; and secondly, to instruct us in our parenting and caring. Many of us, having reflected in such a way, have deliberately decided to either delete or repeat behaviours and attitudes we've inherited from our caregivers. As an ally to a gender-expansive child, surveying this inner territory is essential reconnaissance.

Our identity is collaged throughout our lives, though the foundational years are absolutely critical ones. When we recognise and accept this, our vigilance on behalf of our kids will increase accordingly. We make no apology for monitoring the actions of other people to protect our child's fledging sense of self. The identity of our child or young person is an evolving early work in progress, a collage where the colours, forms and features are not yet fixed, the textures and trimmings not yet decided upon. A major part of our role is to oversee this unfolding and to ensure, as far as is possible, that nothing sabotages it. Self-knowledge combined with agency, will help us to achieve this.

Self-knowledge limits the harm of self-ignorance

Learning to tell ourselves the truth can feel scary and even terrifying on some occasions. But if we distance ourselves from self-knowledge, it's not without a cost: in doing so, we're choosing to stay attached to our self-ignorance (self-ignorance about why we hold the attitudes, values and beliefs that we do, or, worse still, not knowing what these might be in the first place). In such a vacuum, many people mimic the most outrageous voices they hear in a vicarious attempt to be 'someone' themselves. But when self-ignorance is coupled with power, then we have good reason to be highly disturbed. In some circumstances self-ignorant people can rampage dangerously. They mete out all manner of violence and will often do so from a position of arrogant entitlement. This violence isn't necessarily physical. It can be written into a policy or procedure. It can evict a family from their apartment or slam the door of a cell in someone's face. It can deprive women of medical treatment or sack an individual from their job. It can put a child onto the street. James Baldwin gives poetic voice to this: 'It is certain, in any case, that ignorance, allied with power, is the most ferocious enemy justice can have.'[1]

For many of us, in our homes and in our relationships, our motivation to stay attached to self-ignorance is functional rather than vindictive. If my behaviour has hurt someone I can avoid feeling distress through the psychological mechanism of avoidance. In plain words, I can look the other way. All of us have done this at one time in our lives or another. And, we must name it for what it is: cowardice. We are shielding ourselves from emotional pain at the expense of someone else suffering, perhaps even our child. I recently spoke with Brock Dumville, Senior Crisis Service Manager at The Trevor Project, the leading national organisation providing crisis intervention and suicide prevention services to LGBTQ youth in the United States. Brock has interacted with hundreds of young people who are attempting to recover from the traumatic outcomes of their parent's denial:

> What happens is that the feelings of adults who are caught up in avoidance often 'snowball' and this results in them sending their kids to more and more destructive therapies, including conversion programs that sometimes use shock therapy – literally torturing someone to be, quote unquote, 'normal', which is very obviously dangerous and doesn't work.

---

1   Baldwin, J. (2007) *No Name in the Street*. New York, NY: Vintage. Also available at www.brainyquote.com/citation/quotes/quotes/j/jamesaball124903.html, accessed on 06 September 2017.

And by 'normal', of course, parents mean someone like them. Someone they recognise themselves in. But that someone isn't them and the damage done by this process is often hard, and sometimes impossible to undo. Tragically for some young people, escape rather than survival becomes their most consuming goal. Whatever the detail of your family's story, please understand this. You are responsible for how you manage your thoughts, feelings and behaviours. I recognise this is a weighty thing to say, especially if you're feeling distraught or damned by your situation at the moment. I would be patronising you if I didn't make my point explicit here. We all get to choose our attitude in any given set of circumstances. Projecting your discomfort, upset and disappointment onto your child isn't okay; nor should anyone else be permitted to do so. It's better to take part in this entire conversation with ourselves than to remain mute. If we choose otherwise, then we cannot claim victimhood when things go badly. It's a major part of our job as parents and caregivers to deal with our own emotional and psychological fallout, and not use our children's psyches as a dumping ground for it. None of us are exempt from making decisions we later regret, or from behaving in ways that leave us feeling ashamed at times – myself included. The important thing is that we find the courage to tell ourselves the truth about it, and, as kindly as we're able to. This puts us back in the adult realm of taking responsibility, and taking responsibility gives us choice. It requires a lot of guts and a good dose of humility to model honesty and vulnerability in this way. I'd encourage you to keep travelling in that direction.

How do we gain self-knowledge?

Mainstream culture hardly ever directs us towards investigating our own personal universe. If you did a quick scan now of the television channels you're subscribed to, the music you listen to or the online entertainment you use, what percentage is properly concerned with developing your inner life? These outlets showcase the world but rarely include anything to help you discover the internal one you inhabit. Western culture, predominantly, is extrovert. It's all 'out there' and characterised by one word in particular: 'fast'. And when we're all travelling at such speed, it's easy to overlook that we're being driven by different factors.

Our individual self carries around its own 'map of the world'. This map is how we make sense of everything that's happened to us, and I mean everything from conception onwards – nature, nurture and the trillions of interactions that merge in each human being to create a unique whole. By the time we're adults, much of the map is bolted down, which can become problematic if we find ourselves on ground we don't recognise. Or, as is repeatedly the case, we assume that everyone's map is a replica of our own. If we're wedded to either of these positions, they will jeopardise our child's welfare over time.

Developing our self-knowledge means that we get curious about our map: Why do we think, feel and react as we do? Why are we drawn to some people and not others? Why do we consistently overreact in certain situations, procrastinate in others, take too many risks or never take any? Why, indeed, does our child's gender expression provoke such strong responses in us? To mix metaphors, when we commit to self-knowledge we have got out of the driving seat of our life and begun to look underneath the bonnet. We want to learn about the various parts we find there, how they interact and impact on each other and if any of them need tweaking or changing. Skilling our self up in this way means we're able to intentionally direct our life and not simply drive through it on automatic pilot. When we commit to self-knowledge as an ally, we're committing to our child. We're honouring their experience as well as our own. We stop insisting that everyone – including, and perhaps especially, our gender-expansive child – use the map we're the author of.

Self-knowledge develops according to the depth of the attention we give to it and this, ultimately, determines whether our personal map of the world will be large-scale and detailed, or small-scale and limited. A large-scale, detailed map encompasses both a breadth of perspective and a concentration on the specific. This is a model we can usefully apply to ourselves: are you seeing in detail or deleting what you don't want to see? Where do you gain a breadth of perspective from? How can you assess whether who you think you are and how other people see you are the same? Let's look at this much more closely now.

Active enquiry

Active enquiry is the underpinning attitude we want when it comes to gaining self-knowledge. For our purposes, we're shaping this enquiry around our role as an ally. The Matrix is terrain we're now re-claiming for ourselves and this attitude is equivalent to the sturdy boots we need in order to do so. Any other footwear will tear at the seams after the first strenuous climb. Active enquiry is to do with forward momentum. You're putting some effort in to discover something new or to make sense of something old. Many of these steps can be taken in solitude, some of which I've referenced already. Practices such as reflective journal writing, contemplative walks, meditation, prayer, and reading to expand awareness require little more than our own company. There are many ways to travel into self-knowledge and away from self-ignorance. What separates the devout student of this process from the serious one, though, is a commitment to asking for feedback. Such a person knows that deep self-knowledge is crucially dependent on the perspectives of other people too. If we're unwilling to receive feedback as information, then what we know about ourselves will forever be limited. On the other hand, when we engage with constructive comments (alongside the fluffy stuff we all love to receive), then important discoveries await us. What we do with them depends on the decisions we make about whether we feel the feedback is valid or not. And that's often when the boots on our feet will really have some work to do.

When it comes to self-knowledge, especially self-knowledge in the realm of being an ally, an essential person to go to for feedback about how you're doing is your child. It's a brave move to make. I say this because children can be fearless in their frankness with no intent to hurt. And our children know us better than most other people do, so this puts us, as adults, in a vulnerable position. Yet this sort of dialogue is essential. We may have a view of ourselves and our actions that's inconsistent with how our children perceive us.

For instance, I want you to imagine Tania, a loving long-term foster-carer to Acer, a gender-expansive foster-son. Tania believes she's now being fully supportive of Acer's journey. She's read a great deal about gender identity, she's listened intently to her foster-child, ceased making inappropriate comments and can now tolerate gender diversity in a way that once felt impossible to her. Friends admire her attitude and comment that she's an example to them of inclusive parenting. Tania knows she's made progress and, mostly, doesn't require thanks for it. If anyone were to ask Tania to describe herself as a foster-mum to a gender-expansive young person, she might sincerely say 'open, supportive and available'. But this isn't Acer's perspective, which is often hard for him to bear. He appreciates that Tania has made a great effort to change since he came to live in her home. Acer values the freedom that she allows him to choose most of his own clothes now, and rarely makes excuses about his appearance anymore. He knows from the Internet that many other kids don't have things as easy as him. But Acer can't completely depend on his foster-mum as an ally. He needs his gender identity to be fully accepted by her and not only tolerated. Acer registers Tania's frown when he talks about joining a local LGBTQ group for teenagers; or how she sometimes makes a 'joke' that 'he can't make his mind up' if she thinks Acer can't hear her. He knows their conversations are conditional on Tania not getting 'too upset', and when to keep out of the way if certain friends of hers come over. So even though Tania identifies as a fully fledged ally, her self-knowledge is stagnating in this area. She's taken on board a lot of affirmative feedback, without staying engaged in the bigger conversation between herself and her foster-son. And now she's in the position of 'not knowing what she doesn't know', without being aware of it. The mark of the Matrix is subtle and we often need others to point it out to us. Acer could help Tania take another step on the journey, if she's able to listen to everything he yearns to share with her. Her foster-son may find the emotional resources to approach Tania, but this puts the responsibility on his young shoulders, again. So what might Tania do to change this situation for herself? What can you or I do to ensure our self-knowledge continues to deepen and expand, and, in doing so, continues to serve the best interests of our child?

Self-awareness: Why is it important to you as an ally?

Self-knowledge and self-awareness are like two paddles – one positioned either side of our life, guiding its direction. They work in conjunction with each other and with the surrounding elements. I think of self-knowledge as one paddle, which dips into many currents including the past, and self-awareness as the other paddle, which dips only into the present. As a pair they strengthen, consolidate and sustain each other. Together they have the potential to lead us to a place that exists beyond our cultural conditioning.

Self-awareness is the main channel that irrigates and expands self-knowledge and agency. It starts to evolve in us from a very young age as we observe ourselves in action and learn to think about our thought processes. As adults, this process is a 'taken for granted' dimension of our existence, which is switched 'on' or 'off' in us at different times. You might notice, for instance, that your concentration has lapsed as you're driving along a dark and unfamiliar road, and you suddenly bring your attention to ensure safety. Or perhaps you're having lunch with a friend who, with flushed cheeks, tells you that she's just been promoted. You notice a surge of feeling in your body, and a fork of envy twist your gut. In almost the same moment, you register that the emotion is to do with your sense of inadequacy in work, and not your friend's success. Or, it may be that though your days are happily 'settled', you notice a part of yourself also longing for some disorder amongst the tidiness. In fact, often it's a crisis situation that breaks the spell of our surface habitual awareness. Then we find ourselves looking at our life as though it's wearing clothes that belong to someone else, only we'd never perceived this before. My point is this: understanding that you already have the capacity to step out of your 'ordinary' self and watch your thoughts, feelings and behaviour is the beginning of self-awareness.

Self-awareness leads to choosing overreacting

Our mind is usually a crowded place. Most of the time we're either logging, categorising, analysing, chasing, censoring or trying to subdue our thoughts. What we value can sometimes get lost or misplaced in the throng, particularly if external pressures are brought to bear on us too. Cultivating self-awareness keeps us in touch with our inner life. It safeguards our values, our sense of direction and our purpose. Building our capacity to pause, witness ourselves and reflect will keep us grounded in what's true for us. The more 'aware-full' we become, the better our intuition will be when something feels 'off' inside ourselves or outside. This awareness will offer the opportunity to navigate back into the flow of what feels right for us or our child.

When you're parenting against the gender grain, staying 'present' and available to yourself in this way will require concentrated effort. It's worth it, because pausing, witnessing and reflecting naturally lead to choice. And choice is a vital commodity in the empowerment stakes. When we stay mindful, we recognise that options are always available to us: we don't 'have to' be driven by our feelings, moods or the demands of other people; we're not a victim of our circumstances.

This is the difference between reactive and proactive folk. Reactive people lose sight of their values when the pressure's on, while proactive ones bring them into sharper focus. Reactive people make excuses for themselves and proactive people take responsibility. We learn to be proactive through a commitment to self-awareness. It will hold a mirror up to us, and hold us accountable. But please don't mistake it for a hard taskmaster – it isn't. Self-awareness equips us to cut a path through the undergrowth of confusion, self-interest, guilt and ignorance that all of us are subject to in a human life. It will locate us back in our values if we permit it to do so. Through the process of mirroring our behaviour, and offering choices in response to it, self-awareness builds muscle in us: the muscle to pause, witness and reflect in a moment; the muscle to model qualities that will sustain our kids into the future; the muscle we need to become positive choice-makers in our own lives, and in the lives of our gender-expansive children.

Self-awareness leads to 'parenting on purpose'

Mindfulness has been called the practice of 'paying attention on purpose'. Given this, I think we can usefully extend it to 'parenting on purpose' as well. In other words, when we choose to expand our natural capacity to 'watch' ourselves through mindfulness, this strengthens our capacity to parent with our purpose always in mind and heart. To 'parent on purpose' this way means that you are in the best possible position to relate healthily to your child and to advocate strongly for them. When we stay aware of what's going on inside of our own private world at any given moment, we stay capable of influencing what's going on around us, and around our child. Let me give you an example: Last summer I was on a train with Ruby. At the time she still went under the name of Ruben, even though she'd recently socially transitioned and presented as a girl in the world. Ruben and I were going away for a few days and she was excited and happy. Her energy created a small force field of joy around her and I watched as people were drawn into it. The man sitting behind us waved at Ruben through the division between our seats. Then a young woman, with a rucksack on her back and a book in her hand, caught Ruben's eye as she passed through the carriage. She stopped and began to chat with her. Ruben reciprocated, her eyes shining and her speech fast as she told her how much she loved being on a train with Nanny, and Mummy was driving down with her sister and soon we'd all be together, and our holiday house had a balcony overlooking the beach. The woman explained that she was a student teacher and was on her holidays too. She asked Ruben about school and what subjects she liked learning about. A balloon of anxiety gradually began to inflate inside my chest as the conversation between the two of them continued. Finally, the young woman moved on and I cuddled up next to my grandchild. Ruben resumed her watch for the first glimpse of sea through the window and I sat with my feelings. A sharp mixture of regret and relief rose up in me. I'd been cold towards my fellow passenger and grateful that she'd quickly left us alone. I realised I'd avoided eye contact and had turned my knees away from her too, even as I grasped Ruben's warm fingers in my own. As the pressure in my shoulders softened and my breathing slowed down, I began to track the self-talk I'd been subject to.

'I wish she'd go away.'

'What can I do to get Ruben's attention?'

'Shall I pretend we have to make a phone call?'

'What if she asks Ruben his name?'

'How can I make her leave?'

'What if she sits down?'

Tuning in and listening to my self-talk in this way, of itself opened up a space I could step into, away from my considerable anxieties. From that space I recognised the 'hot thought' immediately, the one that had held its fingers around my throat. 'What if she asks Ruben her name?' This was the thought that I'd been joisting with the entire time the woman had been standing next to us. The reason was clear to me: I didn't want Ruben to absorb any confusion that might have been reflected on the young teacher's face. I didn't want her to internalise any suggestion of 'wrong'. As soon as all these elements surfaced into my awareness, the tension in my body began to completely melt away. The 'fight or flight' hormones inside me began to subside and I could think more clearly. This was a vital link in the chain. My brain wasn't in 'threat' mode any longer, so I could reflect on what had happened. To ensure that I'd be able to do this calmly, I also made a conscious decision to not 'get lost in the story' of what had just taken place. If I'd continued to replay it and berate myself, then my energy would have been sapped further. At this point, I was able to switch over to strategic thinking to create a plan should this situation arise again. And sure enough it did.

An hour or so more into our trip and Ruben was standing next to me as we waited in a queue to buy a snack from the on-board café. Another woman gazed down at her for a long moment and quietly said to me, 'What lovely eyes she has.' Then she lightly touched Ruben's ponytail and asked, 'What's your name?' Within a beat I answered for her, using the nickname I've called Ruben since she was a toddler, which coincidentally happens to be gender neutral. The woman looked at me, slightly unsure, and I smiled and repeated it. Ruben beamed back at her too because the exchange seemed entirely normal to her. We bought our drinks, said a friendly goodbye and returned to our seats.

Becoming aware-full moment by moment, isn't given to us by right, it has to be earned. Initially, in the example above, I wasn't aware-full. I was quickly slipping into reactivity because I wasn't paying enough attention to my anxiety, which was expressing itself through my body language and self-talk. My mindfulness practice only significantly kicked in after the 'threat' had passed by. When I did pause and witness myself, my reactive behaviours fell away and I became present. In becoming present, I was able to consciously register my fears for Ruben's well-being. In doing so I could exercise choice and strategise around her needs. I became proactive. And what this all amounted to was safeguarding Ruben's emerging sense of self. And safeguarding myself from panic, uncertainty and regret.

Self-awareness leads to self-compassion

When self-awareness is welcome in our lives as a positive, affirming force, it will lead us to self-compassion. Our kindness won't only be reserved for people other than ourselves. Too often, far too often, as parents and caregivers we end up scraping the bottom of the bucket in an effort to nurture ourselves, only to find there's nothing left in it. And we go hungry, again. This isn't sustainable. We have to include our own mental and emotional health in the wider picture of our family situation, or the consequences could be dire. Self-awareness precedes self-care. As allies, we're in for the long haul, whether our kids remain gender expansive or, one day, identify fully with the gender they were assigned to at birth. Either way, when we become more self-aware, we notice what we need far more readily. We might only be able to meet these needs partially, be that a few quiet hours in a park instead of a weekend away, or taking a long bath instead of a swim in the sea. But these actions will signal to our struggling selves, 'I see you,' and this is why we still feel nurtured, irrespective of our budget or diary commitments. 'Nurture' is a verb, an action word. As we repeatedly notice our needs through our developing self-awareness, and meet them the best way we can, a positive spiral gets initiated deep within us. This spiral will generate spark, energy and resolve for the road opening out in front of us.

Self-esteem: Why is it important to you as an ally?

When self-knowledge and self-awareness are the two paddles either side of our life that guide our direction of travel, healthy self-esteem will eventually sit at the helm. When self-esteem is anchored in our depths, it's powerful. It will be the harbour we sail out of and the port we return to, even when the seas are rough. It will steer us to our destination in steadfast and ingenious ways. Good self-esteem enables us to both see opportunities and to take them. It sustains us as individuals and, significantly, strongly influences how others respond to us.

Learning to trust our own wisdom

Implicit in building self-esteem is building trust in our own knowing. Learning to trust in our own wisdom isn't always easy, especially when individuals, systems and segments of society mark out our parenting as wrong, and mark our child out as disordered in some way. You know, as I do, that parenting a child with a difference – any difference – comes with extra challenges. When that child has a difference that is regarded by many as unacceptable, the challenges can multiply. I saw a post on Facebook recently about parenting children with additional learning needs. One of the little yellow stickers held up to the camera said: 'You will become an army for your child.' I believe this. I believe that most parents will become an army for their child if their child's needs demand it, even if those same parents sometimes feel confined to the barracks of their own insecurities. To be an army requires strength, discipline and the drive to keep pushing on, no matter what. Whatever outer resources we have at our disposal, without these inner ones, their impact will be limited.

Self-esteem is formulated along two intersecting lines. The first is how competent we judge ourselves to be, and the second is how much worth and value we intrinsically feel. If we're fortunate enough to score highly in both these categories, then we're fortunate indeed. Someone in this position respects and appreciates themselves and, importantly, feels entitled to take up space in the world. People with high self-esteem usually enjoy high rank too, as it generates a lot of privileges. If your self-esteem is lower than you'd like it to be, then building inner trust can feel like an unrelenting slog. You may even have established a self-defeating pattern of attacking the most desperate and vulnerable parts of yourself. Inevitably, the civil war within you will lead to painful consequences, not least unremitting stress. When we're stressed, we react to people and events and fail to notice our own feelings. If this persists and we begin to overreact, this means we're acting without thinking at all. And this loss of control means we're then at the mercy of external events. When we've 'lost' our centre in this way, we're essentially surrendering our power to think and act on our own behalf. This exposes us, and potentially our children, to the line of fire in any conflict situation. Reactivity is *always* a warning light telling us to stop.

If any of these words are resonating with you, I'd encourage you to acknowledge those feelings now. Please don't exhaust your fragile energy with recriminations or regret. Instead, gather it around yourself and whisper something loving into your own ear. Set an intention to participate in your own rescue and then begin to explore how. When we find our way back to ourselves, we find our way forward. I encourage you, strongly, to seek assistance. This help may come in the form of personal therapy, a support group, an inclusive spiritual community, a helpline or a course in assertiveness, for instance. As the saying goes, 'If you want to eat an elephant, then start with a teaspoon.' Think manageable. Be brave. Take one small step. Then take another. Keep going. The very good news is that self-esteem doesn't belong to the chosen few, it isn't at a fixed level in your life and it can improve. The same applies to your child.

Inner trust is essential to parenting a gender-expansive child wisely; to navigating the territory their gender journey has taken us into. Inner trust is the spirit level we use as an ally to discern if something, or someone, isn't aligned to our child's wholeness. I believe all of us carry our own source of wisdom, although most of us need to find our way back to it. There was a time in my life, during a major personal crisis, when I was compelled to take this daunting journey. I'd been depressed for about a year and my psyche had become dominated by a harsh critical figure. My self-esteem was reduced to a shattered dish full of grey ash. The figure seemed to take pleasure in my downfall and plagued me relentlessly. Everything I did or said was measured and found wanting against perfection. This aspect of my psyche gave me hell and I gave her a name: Harridan. I caught her essence in my journal: 'I try to stand up, but she pushes me down and skewers my cheek with the heel of her shoe.' After finding these words in myself I set about deposing her. Through a combination of sustained inner work, life changes, spiritual nurturing and emotional support, the battle I had with this internal figure came to an end. It transformed first of all into mediation between us and, finally, into a peace agreement. She still shows up occasionally, though, happily, very rarely these days.

I'm sharing this experience because, traumatic as it was, it changed me for the better. The pain and loss I experienced broke me open into a deeper consciousness. Through it I finally learnt, as an adult, to subdue my ego. Only then could I recognise and honour my own wisdom. I came to understand that the path to integrity lay in being accountable to myself first and foremost, in honouring my own truth, even if it was unacceptable to people around me. I'm not suggesting here that I now live permanently in some sort of enlightened state – that would be ludicrous; or that my life is picture-perfect because I never make any mistakes – far from it. What I *am* saying is that I now have a deep internal resource I can depend on. And I'm not exceptional in this regard – not at all. Some people call this part of their consciousness their 'Higher Self', 'God', their 'Inner Witness' or 'Source'. Some people relate to it as a feeling state within their body and don't name it at all. Honour the 'still small voice' at the centre of your being, even if it doesn't sound like the one you've been trained to 'hear' from an outside authority. What counts is that we cultivate a connection to our own truth; that we pay attention to it. We listen, for even the faintest echo of our own wisdom, then orientate our whole self towards it: body, mind and soul.

Why do we doubt ourselves and flounder in the context of professional engagement?

Parenting is not socially recognised as work. It comes with meagre status, there are no financial rewards built in and you'll rarely, if ever, be asked to do a presentation on your role. Yet anyone who dedicates themselves to being the best parent or caregiver they can be is setting in motion a chain of events that will reverberate positively for generations to come. This absence of recognition is not incidental. It evolved out of a context that labelled childcare as 'women's work' and shoved both parties, women and children, to the side. The legacy of devaluing the labour of women means that many still experience a gradual loss of social and professional confidence when they become mothers. And this also applies to some fathers if they take on a full-time childcare role. If women in particular resume paid employment, then conflicted feelings may sabotage their confidence at home and at work because they feel as though they can't be fully present in both places. And, unfortunately, informal employment practices such as 'present-ism', the expectation that people who want to 'get ahead' arrive early and leave late, erodes peace of mind further. Common dynamics like these, plus an acute lack of positive social mirroring that validates childcare as a worthwhile role, are social issues and not individual failings. In fact, they are window panes we can look through to the Matrix. These interrelated components don't disappear when parents find themselves in a consultation room. In such circumstances, our own feelings about relative power, privilege and rank will inevitably flood to the surface.

The professional – let's say a psychologist – will have letters after their name that you don't have after yours. It's likely you'll be meeting on their 'territory', and the psychologist and their colleagues will be fluent in their own language. You'll step into this unfamiliar arena with your beloved child, holding onto your best hopes and, often, beset with fears. Despite the clinician's best intentions, they still may not recognise the impact that their everyday world might have on your family.

Parenting from a place of healthy self-belief

I want to encourage you to own your authority as a parent because, to a great extent, you're an expert on your child. And, it's important that I qualify exactly what I mean by that statement. None of us become experts on the children we care for automatically, coincidently or through osmosis alone, so this title is conditional. To authentically claim it, I guarantee you will have applied yourself to bonding, building, maintaining and shielding the relationship you have with your child, for your expertise to be worth anything at all. Our best, most reliable knowledge about our kids, our skills in relating to them, our insights and intuitions will, necessarily, have been forged in the crucible of unconditional love. Believe me, to parent in this way is a full-time occupation, as many of you will know. There will be potholes in the road, signposts missing and detours where we're not expecting them. Many times we'll spin the same roundabout and many times we'll find ourselves reversing out of dead-ends. Finally, little by little, we'll start to gain some ground and begin to feel like we know what we're doing – at least for part of the time.

Then something unexpected might happen. Our boy tells us he's really a girl, or our girl tells us she's really a boy. Our son says his gender's a mystery to him, or our daughter tells us hers is a changing landscape. A niece, a nephew, a foster-child or grandchild might express their gender in such a way that our temples pound as we try to understand what they're communicating to us. Before too long, dilemmas start to present themselves, conflicts begin to ensue, advice is given and fingers start to wag. Maybe tongues too. It's very easy to give up your authority as a parent and caregiver when you're experiencing all, or some, of these pressures. It's hard to maintain belief in your decisions when they're being made in a context that may be utterly unfamiliar to you. And this, perhaps, is where we, as parents and caregivers, are most vulnerable. We begin to look around for support and advice, and that's a smart thing to do. It's also a risky thing to do because then we have to discern who is worthy of this role. We may even find ourselves looking for an 'expert' to 'tell' us what to do. It's easy to panic at this impasse or jump towards the safety of what's known over what isn't. We must be careful here. Gender variance has been labelled 'unnatural' in Western cultures for a very long time and pathologised as such – treated as a sickness or disorder that must be remedied. So-called 'reparative therapies',[2] which are designed to 'cure' children of their gender discrepancies, are not yet a relic of the past. The Golden Thread your child has in their grasp may lead to a lot of professional involvement or very little. As you seek the right support team for your particular family and circumstance, trust your gut. Professionals who see themselves first and foremost as guides, rather than experts, will be your best allies. These people, who may indeed be experts in their field, use their knowledge and skills *in service* to others. And you will feel this in your bones when you meet them. Trust that feeling.

Self-forgiveness: Why is it important to you as an ally?

Parenting a child who colours outside of gender lines can feel like rafting in white water without a safety jacket on. Sometimes the waves hit from every direction and adrenaline runs high. One rapid might be the stormy self-realisation that you acted on a bias you didn't know you had. Another could be a gender siren blasting in your head because a 'rule' has been broken. You might have allowed the dogma of other people to govern the course the boat takes. Or a rapid may capsize the boat altogether if you insist on conformity over conversation with your angry child. Then again, you may even have refused to get into the raft in the first place. Instead, you crouch

---

2   For a full discussion of the impact of 'reparative therapies', see: Murchison, G., Adkins, D., Conard, L. A., Ehrensaft, D. *et al.* (2016) *Supporting and Caring for Transgender Children.* Available at http://hrc-assets.s3-website-us-east-1.amazonaws. com//files/documents/SupportingCaringforTransChildren.pdf, accessed on 14 July 2017.

on the bank, heels stuck in the mud, blasting out instructions and demanding obedience.

If the river's heaving like this, or even choppy, then some decisions you've made will have been because of fear, panic and ignorance. And some interactions you've had will have been soldered with fury and disrespect. When the rapids are exhausted, alongside you and your family perhaps, it will take a lot of integrity to review the damage that's been done. At times such as these, human beings have a large array of psychological tools at their disposal to avoid feeling shame and regret: denial, wishful thinking, false hope, self-deception and a powerful instinct to repress our true feelings. Unfortunately, many of us use these tools with great finesse. In this circumstance, I encourage you to put them down, even if it means you need to seek help to do so.

Behaviour that parents and caregivers regret has the capacity to keep inflicting harm if it isn't addressed all the way through to forgiving oneself for it. Please don't take this option. Not only will it continue to impact negatively on your child, your unresolved feelings will keep impacting negatively on you. When we repress something that keeps telling us it wants to be expressed, this will come at a cost: depression, anger and unhappiness that won't go away. This process significantly depletes our energy. It's the metaphorical equivalent of managing your life with only one hand, because the other is always holding a lid down somewhere else. All of this is counterproductive anyway because feelings leak out and we often use behaviours such as overeating, drinking too much alcohol, overwork or even exercise to numb the feelings we don't want to admit to. Then we become even more emotionally unavailable. It's a vicious circle that eventually will spiral around a central point of self-loathing. We must risk self-forgiveness. If we don't, our children will surely pay for it, one way or another.

Self-forgiveness isn't a pat on the back and a 'there, there' response to our actions because now we feel upset about them. Self-forgiveness starts with getting so close to the jaws of our wrongdoing that we can inhale its breath. It means taking responsibility with no excuses and expressing our remorse. It means making amends and being determined to do so. It means humility and then setting a clear intention to do better next time. And, when all of this is completed, it means letting go of our guilt, even if the letting go takes many attempts. I hope, as I write these words, that you can hear the message I want to convey in them. All of us make mistakes as parents, and what we do afterwards still counts. Wrongdoings can help generate relationships if we're able to process what happened with others. You may have made decisions, taken actions and spoken words you've later regretted; you may have imposed something on your child you sincerely believed was for the best; you may have blamed them and withheld love in response to the situation you perceive their gender nonconformity has put you in. But continual avoidance will only rob you of each other. These are hard things to acknowledge, yet honouring your growing self-awareness requires you to. I recognise too, that some of you reading this book may be estranged from your child. You may feel the opportunity to put things right is lost to you. I don't pretend to know what this must feel like. I do know, however, that people exist who've taken a wound – either one that was inflicted on them, or one they inflicted on someone else – and have dedicated themselves to transforming it into a gift. One of these stories, from the LGBTQ community, may be just the story you need to seek out for yourself right now. Who knows? In time your story of hurt and healing may become part of this catalogue and bring hope to other people. If you've pledged yourself to be an ally, then there's always a new beginning, no matter the history that you bring with you.

The work you're doing on self-awareness and the cumulative self-knowledge you're building as a result of this will support you into the future. Self-forgiveness, which follows the process I describe above, for something you did in the past – be that five minutes, five months or five years ago – is equally important. My hope is that you'll release what's unforgiven in you, put right what you're able to, and find peace in yourself once more.

CHAPTER 9

DISMANTLING THE MATRIX

Withdrawing our allegiance

The Cambridge Dictionary contains the following entry:

Allegiance: loyalty or support for a ruler, country, group or belief. From the Old French word, Liege, meaning 'lord and master'.

We can, and must, forgive ourselves for forming an allegiance to the Matrix. None of us are exempt from the long fingers of its manipulation. Culturally, we're seduced into becoming dependent on gender norms, and then we form entrenched and compulsive habits around them. Eventually, we're so hooked in to this formula that we act as though our very survival depends on it. Until our child began to play at, and then edge across its borders, it's likely our allegiance to the Matrix lay unprovoked, like a sleeping ogre. As long as it wasn't poked or prodded, we could tiptoe safely around it and not even realise we were doing so. But the ogre has stirred and we, as allies, have determined to confront it.

Setting our will-to-do-good
The power of the independent human will is an awesome thing to behold. Whenever we see dramatic evidence of it, people are mesmerised. Truly, a concentrated will can achieve astonishing

outcomes. And it isn't only a resource bequeathed to a selected few, the preserve of the 'chosen ones'. It's a resource we all have access to and can consciously develop.[1] But attaining a strong will, of itself, isn't enough. Indeed, such a force can be malignant, as history teaches us. It's only when we commit to aligning the will with our highest principles, that its transformation into the 'will-to-do-good' begins.

As an ally you must be able to assert 'I *will* withdraw my allegiance to the Gender Matrix' and then collaborate with your will to fulfil this intention. There is no other place to begin. Without the will to make something happen, there isn't a way forward. If we're unable to focus our will sufficiently, then we're not only at the mercy of our own impulses and whims, we're at the mercy of other people's. And our children will be dragged through this ambivalence and chaos too. This is not what we choose as allies. We choose to do our inner work so our children can thrive in our company. We choose to build strength and agency through developing the Four Ss: self-knowledge, self-awareness, self-forgiveness and self-esteem. We choose to inhabit our child's reality through the Four Keys of listening, imagination, empathy and courage.

There are stages of willing, from setting an intention to full realisation. And the will's rightful role is to draw on all our internal resources to engineer this process efficiently. At best, this is a rich and creative conversation between all our parts, and not a weightlifting contest that only 'will-power' has been invited to. For our will to do its work, certain conditions need to be present. The first, and most compelling, is that we're in no doubt what our purpose is. We must possess clear-cut clarity about it. My purpose, in writing this book, arose out of a question that burned in the centre of my being: how can we, as parents and caregivers, accept and protect our gender-expansive children? The answer: to become fully fledged allies to them. I'm assuming that this is your purpose too, or you would

---

1   See: Assagioli, A. (1983) *Act of Will*. New York, NY: Viking.

have put this book down a long time ago. As we harness the strength of our will, this purpose will become a concrete reality in our lives.

Sometimes conjuring our will seems effortless. We have no difficulty in making decisions and we see our chosen path through to its natural conclusion. Perhaps such times may more accurately be described as a 'state of grace'. Much more typically, though, the will is recruited, then strengthened through determined action and struggle. This inevitably means that it has to come against obstacles of some magnitude. They may be internal, external, or both, and will resist and repudiate any effort to get past them. And it's this persistent struggle – choosing between our drives, urges, reasons and 'higher' impulses – that's the training ground for developing a will-to-do-good. The alternative is a will that's driven purely by self-interest and selfish motives.

Our decision to withdraw our allegiance from the Gender Matrix may be made only once, or it may be a decision we repeatedly choose. If you struggle, please don't fret; use your energy to persist. As child-inclusive parents and caregivers, the will-to-do-good on behalf of our child is an indomitable force. Trust it. As we exercise the will to do good, we keep our eyes on the prize and we wisely choose one action over another. We survey all our internal resources and strategically channel them to accomplish our purpose. At its deepest core, the will is freedom: the freedom to make choices and to act the way we want to, in accordance with our principles; the freedom to create for ourselves a Gender Matrix that we willingly pledge our allegiance to.

Owning our allegiance

Acknowledging any allegiance is the doorway to comprehending the depth of it. Walk through it, even if you feel as though the ground beneath your feet is unsteady. It most likely is. I'm asking you to step off territory that's been laid down in your own psyche as 'truth'. To do so is a bold act. I'm asking you to make a decision, for yourself, about your allegiance to the Matrix and the addictive habits that support it. This is a radical act. Parents and caregivers know that buying in to it is highly functional for us. In psychological terms it feels as though we're taking out an insurance policy on our child's future, albeit a dubious one. Shredding up the master copy and writing the terms and conditions for ourselves can feel both liberating and very frightening.

Allegiance is, at core, an internal commitment. When we have an allegiance to something or to someone, it brings with it obligations and natural alignments. We've all witnessed, and perhaps even taken part in, ceremonies where swearing allegiance publicly is the centrepiece of the day. Such ceremonies are deliberately designed to embed allegiance as a binding force in the psyche of the person who's making an oath. There's rarely a 'get out' clause, and withdrawing a commitment often comes with severe penalties. Remarkably, given the gravity of all this, we can be conditioned into an allegiance with no conscious awareness of this at all. As children we were enrolled, taught and cajoled into an allegiance to the Matrix. Through absorbing a rigid belief system, and a code of conduct it was risky to step outside of, we participated in pledge-taking. The process of identifying our allegiance is complicated because it's buried deep inside our psyches. There's no way of knowing which part of the brain and body it's occupying, yet occupy us it does.

As I've already shared with you, my own allegiance to the Matrix and low-level addiction to gender conformity leaked through in my initial responses to Ruben. Despite decades of working to undo my own gender conditioning, given a strong enough provocation, it reared up again. The neuroscientist, Cordelia Fine, offers us an insight as to why:

When the environment makes gender salient, there is a ripple effect on the mind. We start to think of ourselves in terms of our gender, and stereotypes and social expectations become more prominent in the mind. This can change self-perception, alter interests, debilitate or enhance ability, and trigger unintentional discrimination. In other words, the social context influences who you are, how you think and what you do. And these thoughts, attitudes and behaviours of yours, in turn, become part of the social context. It's intimate. It's messy. And it demands a different way of thinking about gender.[2]

Until this different way of thinking about gender manifests, those of us schooled elsewhere must continue to un-school ourselves alone. And though it's likely that we'll never fully eradicate our allegiance, we can radically reorganise it.

Confronting our beliefs

Our allegiance to the Matrix is grounded in our beliefs. A belief is a generalisation about ourselves and our world. Its foundations are located in our past experiences, which include our upbringing, how we've modelled significant others, our successes and failures, and the impact of trauma on us. Beliefs are powerful entities that shape our lives in more ways than we can imagine. They can empower or defeat us, expand or limit us. Within a decade of our birth we will have internalised a multitude of them. During our teenage years, in particular, we will have attempted to throw some of them off in an effort to craft our own map of the world. As young adults and then maturing individuals, we will have discarded a few, kept others and created new ones to live by. And yet, despite all of this effort and attention, a set of beliefs, laid down early on in our psyches, persists. The most enduring of these beliefs relate to our 'primary' identities, and sex and gender meet these criteria.

These early beliefs, which govern our thinking, have anchored in them images and associations. This explains why we can often

---

2   Fine, C. (2010) *Delusions of Gender: The Real Science Behind Sex Differences*. London: Icon Books, p.xxvi.

experience an unbidden response to certain stimuli.[3] For instance, for many people the suggestion of 'old' people having sex is unpalatable, even though rationally they have no reason to feel this. But the wriggled nose and queasy expression gives the game away. It's as though old bodies and sexual activity somehow breach an unspoken code of 'decency'. When an image or association, such as this one, is triggered in our minds, it acts like a mental flint that sparks the sex and gender rules we subscribe to. A tranche of automatic thoughts will follow, which we then assume are a 'true' reflection of our feeling.

Unpicking this process is vital to understanding and undoing our allegiance. It exposes it for what it is: learnt. Our beliefs are thoughts, which activate feelings, behaviours and physical responses in us. A child's gender-expansive expression may also trigger us in this way on some occasions. When this happens, the same principle applies: a feeling is arising out of a belief. Stay with it. It's simply material for you to work with, not grounds for a character assassination. These responses may embarrass, shame or dismay us and our instinct, often, will be to deny, rationalise or otherwise distance ourselves from them. We must allow our will to choose a different path for us. Whatever our reaction – whether we concealed it or not – we need to search for the belief that set it in motion. Then we need to stride straight towards it. This is the territory of deepening self-knowledge, and courageous self-awareness is the leading edge of it.

Identifying our beliefs

Cognitive behavioural therapists work from an evidence base that people have a set of 'core beliefs' which exist at a very deep level. They partner clients to dig out negative and inaccurate thought patterns that are impeding their fulfilment in life. Let me emphasise here that core beliefs don't promenade across our awareness waving brightly at

---

3   This principle applies to all our early embedded beliefs about difference, especially those that have a taboo element to them.

us. I'm talking about very subtle states of mind, which require diligent work to uncover. I also want to stress that though as individuals we evolve a unique set of core beliefs, inevitably in shared cultures and religions, overlap and sameness can be expected. Consequently, group rules and norms, establish and sustain a self-referential system around the beliefs we inherit.

Our core beliefs surface out of our depths as a set of assumptions, which can also be described as 'rules for living'. Tracking our assumptions can lead us to the specific beliefs that have given rise to them. These rules frequently take the form of an 'if/then' statement in our minds. Core beliefs, associated with embedded gender templates, might include: *all women want children*, which leads to the assumption that *if* a woman doesn't have kids, *then* she's not a real woman; or, *heterosexuality is normal*, so *if* I don't comply with this, *then* I'm abnormal; or, as is often the case in traditionally gendered domains, *this is a man's job*, so *if* a woman (or gay man) can do this work, *then* I'm not a real man; or, conversely, *this is a woman's job*, so *if* a man is doing it, *then* he must be gay, or, in some extreme cases, *then* he must be a potential abuser. Our core beliefs about children and gender might include: *boys are resilient*, so *if* my son is still afraid of the dark, *then* he's pathetic; or, *girls should dress modestly*, so *if* my daughter doesn't, *then* she's putting herself at risk. This sequence is activated in a fragment of time, even as our intellect trails behind trying to convince us otherwise.

How do I find my beliefs?

Listen to your self-talk. Becoming aware of your self-talk is a major feature of building our self-awareness. All of us have a pretty constant stream of it filtering through our brains at any given moment. You may have heard self-talk referred to as 'fridge noise' – it's 'just there' and so we ignore it. But what we unconsciously say to ourselves often calls the shots and we don't even realise it. As your awareness begins to quicken, you'll learn to differentiate between your thoughts and classify them as positive or negative. Clearly, positive thoughts energise and enthuse us, while automatic negative thoughts, particularly if they're persistent, drain and depress us. As you become more intimate with your self-talk, pay close attention to the language you hear yourself using. Initially, take a 'big picture' approach so you can develop a broad awareness of your habitual 'chatter'. When you hear 'should', 'ought to' or 'have to' in your vocabulary, stand as still as a deer in a clearing when it hears a twig snap in the undergrowth. These words beg the question: 'Who says I should, ought to or have to?' These commands will have their origin in your relationship with someone else or the culture at large. Follow them to their lair. Are you hearing the voice of a parent or caregiver from your childhood? A sibling who bullied you? Are there echoes of a partner who pulled you down? A priest who intimidated you? Or a cultural norm that's so pervasive to challenge, it feels taboo? These questions will, of themselves, begin to loosen the hold of this belief in your psyche.

In amongst all that fridge noise, as it ebbs and flows throughout any given day, is a subset of core beliefs about gender and sexuality that govern your behaviour. Some of these you'll be conscious of and many you won't be. Employ your self-awareness to listen in. Here's a soundbite of what you might hear:

> *Boys shouldn't flutter their eyelashes like that, girls ought to be sympathetic, it's wrong to wear make-up, if she grows up to be lesbian, I won't have any grandkids, I'm not attracted to older women, if my son is transgender he'll have a terrible life, mothers shouldn't breastfeed in public, I couldn't go out with a short man, bi-sexuality is attention-seeking behaviour, boys are boisterous, girls should help, boys aren't sensitive, girls are too sensitive, women are controlling, men are like children...*

In locating these beliefs, we're not trying to convince ourselves whether they're 'right' or 'wrong'. The objective is to notice how well a belief is serving us or not. Beliefs affect our feelings, thoughts, behaviour and physiology, as quickly as any electric shock would. So we need to get into the habit of regularly reviewing our beliefs and interrogating them. Does this belief limit or empower me? Does it create connection or sever it? Does the belief allow for new possibilities or is it inflexible and rigid? If so, then it's inconsistent with the flow of life, which, as you know, is anything but static.

A useful method to determine a belief, as it's operative in the moment, is to ask ourselves this question: 'What must I believe to be behaving or feeling this way?' A light-hearted, though still gendered, example of this comes to mind as I write these words. I was walking with Ruby a few weeks ago and we turned into a busy road that had a lot of vehicles parked on it. Ruby was skipping ahead of me and I watched her long, glossy hair lifting off her shoulders with every little leap she was taking. Then she slowed down, started to walk, and began to tally, out loud, all the cars she came across: Ford, Vauxhall, Citroen, Audi and Skoda. Ruby was feeling delighted that she'd managed to identify so many vehicles before looking at their badges. I found myself feeling more than slightly bewildered for some reason. If I were to have asked myself the question 'What must I believe to be feeling this way?', the answer would have been obvious to me: 'Girls aren't interested in cars.'[4]

How do I change my beliefs?

Through the process above, we'll identify many beliefs that have their origin in our allegiance to the Matrix. As we change one, this will impact on the others. Remember our quartet of cultural bullies – homophobia, transphobia, cisgenderism and sexism? Undermine one

---

4   Synchronicity is an intriguing thing. Days after I wrote this, I met a 71-year-old woman who's had a lifelong passion for mobile mechanical cranes. Her children celebrated her 70th birthday by gifting her a day where she was able to drive one around, receive instruction in manoeuvring it and then get to work! She subsequently shifted tons of rubble herself. All this before she returned to her rural life in Dorset, where she childminds and cleans people's houses locally.

and you undermine them all. As we change one belief, it will impact on the other. However, it will require the best of our will to extract their roots. How we go about this isn't complicated. We challenge the belief through examining its accuracy. And we do this through the power of another significant question: 'What's my evidence for believing this?'

I'm now going to walk you through a method that explains this process. At the end of it, I've included a hypothetical scenario to show how this method works in practice. Depending on how you learn best, you may want to switch between both parts as we go along or continue to read sequentially through it.

Part I: Choose a belief

Scan your unhelpful beliefs about sex and gender and choose one. You may want to head straight for a belief that's obscuring your child behind it in some way, or one that's always on the edge of your awareness that you've never really faced up to before. Or, choose a belief that's good for a practice run, before you hit the high slopes later. When you've made your decision, I want you to rate how much you currently believe in this negative belief on a 0–100 per cent scale, with 0 = not at all, to 100 = completely. Mark it down somewhere. Then ask yourself the significant question: 'What's my evidence for believing this?'

Part 2: Evidence that supports my gender core belief

When we consider supporting evidence, what matters is that we give ourselves permission to register exactly what counts for us. You don't need to have your evidence 'approved' by anyone but yourself. Write everything down. It's irrelevant whether it's 'factual' or not. Don't feel any pressure to justify what you come up with. Just ask the question and allow your thoughts to reveal the answer to you. Dismantling a belief doesn't occur in the realm of the rational mind. Don't censor *any* of the evidence you're coming up with. You may feel dogmatically convinced of your belief, vulnerable or even 'stupid' as you tease out evidence. No matter, stay with the process and go for the emotional jugular. What counts as evidence for you? What's the 'hot thought', the one that *convinces* you this belief is accurate?

Part 3: Evidence that challenges my gender core belief
Now you need to look for evidence that contravenes the belief. Write it all down. Important information: you don't have to be convinced that this evidence is 'true'; you simply have to generate alternative thoughts that counter your negative belief. Again, keep going. Stretch yourself into this stage. It won't be as easy as finding supportive evidence, because that's already been 'installed' in your mind through your existing self-talk. You'll need to keep guiding your mind to think outside of the box. Give yourself time and keep coming back to generating alternative ideas about the existing gender belief you're currently attached to.

Part 4: Reflect on what's different now
Revisit Part 2 and ask yourself what impact generating these new ideas has had on your old core belief? Rate how much you now currently believe in it.

Part 5: Embrace and embed a gender core belief that's positive now
Given all your evidence, for and against, generate a new positive core belief about gender to replace the old negative one. Strengthening a new belief in our minds is normally more effective than trying to 'weaken' an old negative one. But an outdated belief won't just slip away. The new belief must be given a chance to expand into your awareness and take up more space. To achieve this, commit to a two-week programme where, every day, you notice and record evidence that supports your new positive belief.

A father and son story…

Let's imagine a worried dad, Lloyd, who's a single parent to a quiet, gender-expansive ten-year-old son, Carl. Lloyd's been reading this book, and his conscience is calling him to commit fully to being an ally. He's identified a 'hot thought' that's tormenting him, which keeps getting in the way of his commitment. It's one I've listed in the section above: *if my son's transgender then his life will be terrible.* This painful belief is starting to negatively impact on Carl's gender journey, as the thought is getting the better of his dad. After a row about a 'girl's' toy Lloyd threw away, Carl left the room crying and locked himself in the bathroom. He spent a full hour sobbing. No matter what Lloyd said to Carl, he couldn't persuade him to open the door again. Lloyd got scared. He eventually threatened to 'kick the door down' if his son didn't do as he was told. Carl unlocked it and ran past his father and into his bedroom. Lloyd followed him and sat on his bed. Then he placed his open palm on his son's back. In that moment he knew he had to begin to turn things around and do something different. He knew he had to change himself and not his child. Lloyd has a hunch that the terrorising belief has also got something to do with his allegiance, though he can't quite work out how. He rated his current investment in the belief at 95 per cent.

Here's what Lloyd made of the evidence for and against it:

- *Evidence that supports my belief:*
    - There are high self-harm statistics.
    - There are high suicide rates.
    - Carl will need to live a secret life.
    - There is prejudice in my community towards transgender people.
    - He won't find a job if people know.
    - Transgender youth always have mental health difficulties.
    - His aunty and uncle are homophobic.
    - Carl won't find a partner when he's older.
    - My son will be isolated and lonely.

- Policies will discriminate against him.
- *Evidence that challenges my belief:*
  - His grandparents have accepted this possibility already.
  - The school has been proactive in supporting us both.
  - There are lots of visible trans allies and advocates now.
  - I will always love him, no matter what.
  - Lots of people are single and okay with this.
  - I've read research that proves family acceptance is a powerful safety factor.
  - Transphobia is a hate crime that's against the law.
  - He has good friends.
  - Building Carl's self-esteem will help him stay strong and safe.
  - His sister says he's the bravest person she knows.
  - If being transgender is true for him, then this will make him happy.

After taking himself thoughtfully through this process, Lloyd then rated his investment in his negative belief at around 64 per cent. He recognised that there was lots of evidence that suggested his old belief wasn't accurate. He also noticed something about the hot-thought that had been hidden to him before: *if* my son is transgender, *then* his life will be terrible. It was an assumption that was rooted in a dominant core belief. Lloyd's intuition that his old belief somehow reflected his allegiance to the Matrix stirred. When he then asked himself 'What must I believe to think this way?', the answer was self-evident: *only cisgender people can be happy.* This was a real 'a-ha' insight for Lloyd. The new belief he wanted to install seemed obvious: *transgender people can be equally as happy as cisgender people.* Over the next month or so, Lloyd recorded in detail evidence to support this belief. He still had to manage his fear but he wasn't being controlled by it anymore. What transformed his relationship with Carl, though, was Lloyd's willingness and new-found capacity to travel alongside his son to whatever gender destination he might finally arrive at.

Confronting our gendered selves

Most of you reading this book will identify as cisgender. Some of you will be women readers, some of you men. And, no doubt, a number of sexual orientations will be reflected in the readership. Your circumstances, of course, will be as varied and specific as the families you represent. Some of you will have thought a lot about how gender has defined your life, and others will have barely considered the possibility. But there is one thing we can be sure of that unites us all: we are gendered beings and, inevitably, this fact is made visible through our parenting and caregiving.

This came home to me not so long ago, in a sharp and undeniable way. I was attending a family barbecue with Ruby, her sister and her parents. We were all sitting outside in a relative's rambling, wild garden. There were clusters of people around catching up, enjoying the afternoon sunshine and refilling plates of food. Ruby was running about with her cousins and a gaggle of friends, and returning to our table intermittently for a mouthful of pizza. Eventually, their games subsided and she came to join us, all rosy cheeks and with her fringe sticking to her forehead. She collapsed into the chair next to mine, with her legs splayed open. I gently leaned over and touched one of her knees to close her legs, even though she was wearing freshly laundered, pale pink shorts. The instant I did so, I also witnessed myself taking this action. A specific belief had animated my allegiance, though I had no idea in that moment, what it was. As I sat back in my seat, I replayed the internal sequence of events that had prompted my automatic response. The trigger was Ruby's posture. I closed my eyes and tracked backwards into my uncomfortable feelings when she had sat next to me. Then I found it. A core belief had activated a rule for me: women are ladies; *if* Ruby sits like this *then* she isn't being ladylike. What's striking about this example to me now, is that it wasn't Ruby's gender identity that created a discordant note, it was the particular way she was expressing her femininity. I had swapped my cisgenderism for sexism. I was reinforcing highly gendered norms that girls learn early on, as indeed, did I. Those norms, in this instance, include: a) take up less physical space than boys; b) inhibit your body's natural posture; c) conceal any evidence of your genitals; and d) respect is earned through following these rules. Unwittingly, I was still tutoring my grandchild in the manner of the Matrix. I regretted my action, and when Ruby, rested and rejuvenated, took to running around the garden again, I shared with her parents what had been going on for me. We all agreed that no great harm had been done. Ruby is familiar with diversity, and the gender modelling she gets doesn't, thankfully, only depend on me. The unlearning never ceases.

Scrutinising how our personal gender conditioning influences our caregiving puts another dent in our allegiance to the Matrix. When I first began the research for this book, I had an idea that fathers would have a harder time accepting their child's gender difference than mothers. As a woman, I had no direct experience to draw on, obviously. I've learnt that the evidence does suggest that, at least initially, men do struggle more.[5] I was talking to Ruby's dad, Phil, about this recently. My son-in-law is the sort of person who listens more than talks around a dinner table. He rarely raises his voice, laughs easily and cooks perfect roast beef.

> Yes, I do think dads struggle more. But I can't speak for other men can I? For me the fear thing is there. How am I going to protect my child now when she's going to have so much more chance to be exploited, and bullied, and things like that. I've had dreams about having to protect Ruby at school. It's obviously an ongoing thing, feeling fearful about the future and keeping her safe.

I have no doubt that Phil's words will echo with many fathers who have gender-expansive little ones. His greatest concern, as a man, is how to protect his daughter in a world that guarantees less to her

---

5   Ehrensaft, D. (2011) *Gender Born, Gender Made.* New York, NY: The Experiment, LLC, p.109.
    Brill, S. and Pepper, R. (2008) *The Transgender Child.* San Francisco, CA: Cleis Press, p.40.

than to other children. This burden wakes him up at night. Yet his awareness is also a factor that, inevitably, will contribute to keeping Ruby safe. For some children, regrettably, safety within their homes isn't even guaranteed.

As the authors of *The Transgender Child* tell us:

> The gender training we have all been exposed to from the day we were born includes not only exalting the value of heterosexuality, but also interlinking the values of the ideal male with heterosexuality. Thus the message communicated to all of us, but especially to males, is that perceived or actual homosexuality is an affront to true masculinity. This message is often stronger in certain ethnic and religious communities.[6]

As parents, we often view our kids as extensions of ourselves, so our antennae are always seeking evidence to verify this. Typically, we look to the same-sex child to fulfil this emotional wish for either parent. This belief drives many of our caregiving choices and we often use our parent power to engineer a self-fulfilling prophecy on behalf of this agenda. This might look like only facilitating hobbies that we personally relate to, only 'choosing' friends for our kids that we like, or dressing them in clothes that exclusively broadcast our own taste. But playing 'pairs' with our child in this way is a risky business, not least because it invites denial. We may only see what we want to believe, and gamble with our child's fledgling identity in the process. Or, we my rail against what we do see, and violate our relationship with them instead. As one young person told me, reflecting back on his behaviour as a child:

> I was blissfully unaware of what was to come. I was content with my Barbie and my dresses. I would dress up in my gowns, looking

---

6   Brill, S. and Pepper, R. (2008) *The Transgender Child*. San Francisco, CA: Cleis Press, p.35.

in the mirror, comparing myself to Cinderella and Belle, hoping that one day I'd share their long, wonderful hair. My father, like a bulldozer, crashed through my hopes and dreams, he dashed them to pieces. It was then that reality started to kick in.

Stephanie Brill and Rachel Pepper have more to say about the insidious effects of unaddressed homophobia:

> Within this framework, a male child who is gender variant (and thus perceived as gay) threatens the masculinity of his father. What often happens is that the father often blames the mother for somehow causing this. The poison of homophobia within the gender system spreads to the whole family constellation.[7]

Homophobia is *not* a gender-specific issue, either with regard to who perpetrates it, or who it's projected onto. Having said this, males are coerced into the straightjacket of heterosexual masculinity with particular ferocity. For some, tragically, it creates a forcefield of compliance that's so strong, any bid for freedom feels hopeless. Given all of this, it's not surprising if male caregivers particularly, experience early embedded homophobia seeping, or flooding, into their minds. I want to be clear here that this isn't the same thing as homophobia that's unaddressed and destructive. But there's something all of us, as parents and caregivers of all sexes and genders, are wise to remember. One carries a homeopathic dose of the other within it. That's why engaging with our 'gendered selves' is work we must all be prepared to do. I asked Phil about this too. What were his feelings, as a man specifically, fathering Ruben, and now Ruby?

> I did feel loss. 'My boy' is not my boy anymore, and all the hopes I had for what Ruben have gone. There's that realisation and selfish

---

7   Brill, S. and Pepper, R. (2008) *The Transgender Child*. San Francisco, CA: Cleis Press, p.36.

need. But less of a man? No I don't feel that at all. It wasn't so hard really. When you realise that what you're thinking about is what you want, it changes things. I mean, we did have discussions, didn't we? About who she is, what she believes… As soon as we started to listen, it was a lot easier. You could just say, 'You're not wearing that dress,' but that would be a lot more damaging in the long run wouldn't it? If you look at the end game of what you want, a happy person at the end of it, then all these things you're doing, are they helping your child or hindering them? Saying, 'You're not wearing a dress' is damaging to the end game isn't it? So you need to reflect on it: why am I resisting? The dress thing – is it the right decision? So you go down that road and see where it takes you instead of putting up barriers. For me, it's that fear thing again, because you're acknowledging that you're moving down a different path. So, yes, for every resistance, reflect on it.

Withdraw allegiance and increase acceptance

Acceptance takes time. It also takes determination, resolve and a willingness to travel the whole distance home. If you already value diversity, then acceptance will be easier for you. If you value conformity, it'll be more difficult.[8] Every step is meaningful though, and none is insignificant. If you're able to inject some flexibility into your thinking, it will help. As Lewis, the father of six-year-old Andi, whom we met earlier on, told me:

> There are grey areas everywhere. I don't see the world as black or white. Perhaps it's because of my job? I'm quite comfortable with 'it could be this, it could be that' in every decision. I think it's made our experience with Andi a bit less stressful.

---

8   Brill, S. and Pepper, R. (2008) *The Transgender Child*. San Francisco, CA: Cleis Press, p.42.

Our children are brave souls. The Golden Thread of their gender identity is frequently denied, judged, or found wanting in one way or another. And still they persist in holding onto it. Still they tremble before authority figures, small heads bowed and hearts on fire. Still they continue to risk rejection in the bid to be true to themselves, even if they may be confused, unhappy and unsure for some of the time. Goodness knows, the transition from child to teen to adult is hard enough, without additional complications of any sort. But too often the bravery of gender-expansive kids is only construed as rebellious or offensive in certain settings. Primarily because it contradicts strictly held beliefs about what being a man or a woman, means. Does this resonate with you as a parent and caregiver? If so, I can empathise with you.

When my children were young, my then husband and I were central to a church community that we cared about deeply. I had become converted to Christianity when I was 20 because I saw Jesus as radically inclusive. For a time, it seemed as though I'd found a community that embraced and embodied this vision. But a different reality began to emerge as the church grew and gained in prestige. Looking back, what I see now are leaders who sadly became inflated with power and used their rank in controlling ways to maintain their status in the group. The unhealthy entitlement they acted out was clothed in religious garb. Jesus's gospel of unconditional love became replaced with rule-making and fundamentalist opinions. At the time, I was profoundly bewildered, angered and frightened by the changes in our midst. And, of course, the leaders held the trump card: if anyone challenged them, they had dared to challenge God, which was indefensible. In effect, I now recognise that they were selectively distorting our shared belief system to shore up their position. Put simply, they emphasised the scriptures that served their purposes and conveniently ignored the ones that didn't. The whole circumstance, of itself, grieved me terribly, but more was to come. My son Adam's creative energy and his gender expression became a target of disapproval. The arrows came thick and fast: my child was possessed by 'a spirit of homosexuality', he wasn't a 'natural' boy, his actions needed curtailing, he had to be 'delivered'. Throughout all of this, I strove to listen for my own truth. Then people I once counted on as my dearest friends started to desert us as a family. My faith was tarred and feathered in toxic criticism, though some of it was delivered with a 'spiritual' sleight of hand. Finally, at the brink of a breakdown, I made my decision. My conscience, despite the assault it had been subject to, could not align itself with the 'leadership' in the church.[9] Leaving the community we'd been a part of for so long was traumatic; staying would have been choosing spiritual cyanide. For myself, it was a decision to step into the wilderness and trust that God, as I understood such a mystery, would meet me there. I have not been disappointed. It was also a choice to step away from intolerance, bigotry and fear.[10] As a mother, I was choosing an allegiance to my son over an allegiance to 'leaders' who were proselytising on behalf of the Matrix. At that point in my life, I could never have framed it in this way. Now I know better.

Take the first step...

An allegiance to anything or anyone can become a lethal thing if we're unprepared to review our commitment to it. If we doggedly refuse to heed this call when it comes to us, the results can be catastrophic. However we arrive at questioning our allegiance, it has to be done.

---

9   Christianity doesn't have the monopoly on behaviour like this, and neither do all Christians endorse dogma and discrimination. There are many welcoming churches and faith centres that preserve inclusivity and compassion at the heart of their message. For a thorough and accessible discussion of the psychological dynamics that underpin fundamentalism in any religion, I recommend reading Chapter 2, 'It's Not What We Believe It's the Way That We Believe It', in: Bloom, B. (2004) *SOULution, the Holistic Manifesto*. Carlsbad, CA: Hay House.

10   The report of the U.S. Transgender Study found that 19 per cent of respondents who had ever been part of a spiritual or religious community left due to rejection. Forty-two per cent of them later found a welcoming spiritual or religious community elsewhere, p.6 Executive Summary.

And it's scary to do so. The implications of our conclusion will span out in every direction, with no guarantee of consequence. Yet our purpose gives us no choice. As loving, thinking, feeling, evolving adults, we appreciate that our perceptions and awareness will change as we do. We understand that increased knowledge, personal experience and a deepening maturity can all expand our identity. This will include shedding specific beliefs we once strictly adhered to. The poet David Whyte speaks convincingly to the fear that may inhibit us: 'Start close in, don't take the second step or the third, start with the first thing, close in, the step you don't want to take.'[11] The step we don't want to take is the courageous one. The one we want to avoid. The one whose footprints the others will follow in. If we fail to take it, we don't stand still, our avoidance solemnly initiates a different journey altogether. The poet advises us wisely: 'Start with your own question, give up on other people's questions, don't let them smother something simple.' For us, as child-inclusive parents and caregivers, the simple question is the obvious one: will I pledge my loyalty to the Matrix, or to my child?

Changing our position

The Google dictionary includes the following definition:

> *Positioning: put or arrange (someone or something) in a particular place or way.*

To take up a position is to be visible. When our children act outside of the gender binary this is forced upon us, frequently with scant warning and little preparation. Often, at least initially, the position

---

11   Whyte, D. (2014) *River Flow, New and Selected Poems.* Langley, WA: Many Rivers Press, p.360.

you take up is likely to be a reactive one. It won't be measured, considered or representative of your best ideal. It's likely to be messy and inconsistent. It will be fed by your allegiance and, as such, be fraught with tensions you can barely articulate to yourself, let alone anyone else. It may be that, wham, you're in the middle of a normal day when your son shows up wearing his sister's satin tee-shirt and a shy smile. Or your grandson arrives wearing mauve eyeliner or your foster-daughter refuses to wear female underwear anymore. You have a split second before you take up a position on this. What will it be? And how will you communicate it?

Beliefs and behaviour go together

Allegiance is an internal commitment and how we act, or position ourselves, is the outward evidence of it. Withdrawing our allegiance is a private act and the consequences of it will always be public. It's not possible to separate out these two elements; only to change how they interact with each other, which is our work here. For some of us, this process will feel as laborious as an oil tanker turning 180 degrees on the horizon of our lives; for others it's the rapid landslide of a melting ice shelf into the sea. Neither one way nor the other is 'right'. We're all presented with the same choice in the end; we can wish, want or will something. Turning away from our allegiance and changing our position depends exclusively on the latter.

Beliefs and behaviour go together. I resisted accepting that the initial position I took with Ruby – namely, that trying to 'talk her out of' her feelings – had anything to do with an unconscious allegiance to the Matrix. This possibility sorely contradicted my self-image, so my ego didn't want to engage with it. But 'the still, small voice' inside me, persisted in enquiring about whether it was so. My deep commitment to self-knowledge raised its eyebrows. My further encounters with Ruby poked at my self-awareness and made it flinch. I was, effectively, caught between telling myself a lie and telling myself the truth. I chose the latter. My ego shuddered, but I knew at this point, I'd connected to my own inner source of wisdom. Bringing my allegiance into the light of day liberated me. The sky didn't fall in, the birds didn't fall off their perches, and I hadn't failed my grandchild – in fact, quite the opposite. Instead of the vaporous influence of the Matrix veiling my thoughts and feelings, I could now see it for what it was.

This admission took out a pivotal timber that had been damming up my awareness. The fluidity it created propelled me to explore what else was going on, just below the level of my conscious thinking. I soon realised I'd been denying my feelings for another reason, too. And one far more penetrating than pandering to my own ego. An assumption had trapped me in a headlock, which I didn't know how to get out of: *if my feelings are conflicted, then I'm betraying my grandchild.* Betraying Ruby felt intolerable to me, yet that's what my self-talk was accusing me of. My behaviour in response had been to close my conflicted feelings down in an effort to 'neutralise' this rule, and it hadn't worked. As I further excavated this assumption, through practices that support me, such as journal writing, and with people I trusted to 'hold a space' for me, it gave up its parentage. I came to realise that it was the child of a 'master' belief, stamped onto my psyche when I was very young: *I must be loyal to my family 100 per cent of the time.* Examining that belief close up and 'testing' it to see if it was true, with the perspective of an adult, not a child, enabled me to re-evaluate it. I recognised I couldn't 'own' this belief anymore because it wasn't congruent with my personal map of the world. I needed to take action and replace it with another belief: *I am loyal to my family when it feels true and right to me.* As I followed my process, on paper and in courageous conversations, I saw that this new belief invited me to view my conflicted feelings differently. Instead of shutting them up, the implicit invitation was to consider and explore them. Instead of brushing over their traces in denial, I could let go of my guilt and accept them as information. Pretty soon I realised that one set of feelings doesn't discount another. The fact that I felt conflicted about Ruby's gender journey wasn't sufficient reason to convict myself of betrayal. Welcoming all my feelings allowed me to make sense of my behaviour. Finally, this threw into sharp relief one insight in particular: loving Ruby and accepting her weren't the same thing. My love was unquestionable. Acceptance involved a journey that only I could volunteer to go on.

When we acknowledge our fallibility, then we release ourselves from the tyranny of 'excellence is all'. We must be patient with ourselves. And gentle. This process may mean confronting regrets and some of them may be deep ones. Hold tight. Turn and face them all. Those regrets will provide the fuel to power change once you've taken responsibility for them. Be accountable for things you can control and commit to accepting what you can't. This campaign requires every aspect of our self to be engaged with it to achieve success. Keep everything in the circle of your awareness and exile nothing. In this way we can disarm the Matrix of its 'divide and rule' tactic in our psyches and keep our energy free-flowing and strong. When we frame our experience in this way, progress, not perfection, becomes our driving force.

Change and challenge go together

When we commit to changing our position in relation to our gender-expansive child, it is not only an epic act of love; it is heroic parenting. Not least because, no matter how hard we try, we're never going to 'get it right' all the time. That's an impossibility. And yet, our children will witness and benefit from us trying to, even as we flounder, or face opposition. What counts is our dedicated intention. Intention is the thing that stems our distraction and stops us getting blown off course. To set an intention is to be clear about a purpose we've decided upon. When we bring all of ourselves to this process, we're unified internally, not fragmented. And it's this colossal energy that will infuse our actions to accomplish our plan.

As our allegiance wanes and our position changes in direct relation to this, people around us may take a negative view on our evolving stance. Others may support us wholeheartedly. But judgement, sadly, will never be too far away. How can it not be? In honouring your child's right to take such a path, you may be trespassing on the holy ground of someone else's reality. That person may be your partner, parent, employer, religious leader, a school teacher or your best friend. Any or all of whom, depending on their levels of awareness, might believe they're safeguarding your child's welfare too.

This was the situation that Ellen found herself in with her partner, Ted, the caring step-father to her eldest child, Toni. She recalled how things came to a head between the couple, over nine-year-old Toni's insistent request to wear boy's trunks, not her girl's costume, to a forthcoming swimming party:

> Ted kept saying to me, 'Come on, Ellen, you've got to sort this out. You've got to nip it in the bud. You need to step up and show your daughter where the boundaries are.' I had this constant struggle in mind, am I just being a pushover with Toni? Maybe this is all happening because I split up with her dad? Maybe I really need to hear her at the moment? She was really down and I was thinking, 'You shouldn't be like this at your age.' And I had this other thing in the back of my head, 'You don't understand, Ted. I know my daughter.' He was worried about her mental health in the future. So I made the decision that she had to wear her swimming costume. I remember that it left a sour taste in my mouth. I realised it didn't feel right at all. I just knew that I shouldn't have done it. It was more than Toni being defiant. It wasn't about her being defiant. It was about something else for her much deeper than that. In the end, things got so difficult between Ted and me, we went for counselling. He's always joked about his old-fashioned upbringing and that where he's from

they're about three generations behind the rest of the world. He's an intelligent guy and I always knew whatever happened between us, he'd come round to self-reflecting. He's got all that in place. I knew we would get through things, but it would be hard.

Happily, Ellen and Ted were able to process their issues together and now parent more effectively as a team. This, of course, has benefited everyone: themselves, Toni, and their other children too.

Painfully for many children, this isn't always the case, as we know. In some circumstances, judgement may become contorted into an adversarial conflict that's so severe, it damages everyone concerned. Dynamics such as these are, undoubtedly, exhausting and depleting. Ultimately, they may require a third party such as a counsellor, therapist or legal professional to help you move towards a more child-centred solution.

Next, let's factor in the burden of condemnation many parents feel, given the history of gender diversity in modern culture. There are very few cheerleaders and a great many legislators condemning such experience as deviant. We know that culturally, over time, this has resulted in gender diversity being constructed as a 'pathology' – in other words, akin to a disease. It's a very recent phenomenon that other possibilities are emerging into the mainstream. And while it may seem as though suddenly gender diversity is being embraced with open arms, surveys, statistics and personal stories reveal that this is far from the case. There are batteries of 'gate-keepers' in medicine, education, politics, the media, social policy and religious organisations that actively promote heteronormativity to the exclusion of everyone else. Their devotion to the Matrix is fundamentalist in many cases. Small wonder parents and caregivers who are allies to their children find themselves reeling on occasions. So is there a compass point that can orientate us in the teeth of this gale?

My truth versus your truth

I believe in asking myself powerful questions. And there's one I've come to depend on when I find myself divided from, and in conflict with, another person: 'Have I stepped out of *my truth*, or have I stepped out of theirs?' In the grip of tumultuous feelings and heightened emotions, it isn't easy to hold our ground long enough to ask this question. Yet ask it we must. Many of us succumb to the default of conceding out truth because we fear speaking up and thus being visible. When we're visible, we're within reach. And when we're in reach, we're at risk of being harmed. But silence doesn't promise us peace of mind either. It's not an exaggeration to say that this question can be life-changing. Learning to ask and to answer it is the path to freedom.

When you're reaching a decision about whose truth is dictating your behaviour, you'll need to support yourself well. You'll need to invest quality time in active enquiry, listen deeply to yourself and mainline your courage. You must endeavour to keep the Four Ss within sight. You have receptor sites for truth inside your own being, which include head, heart and 'gut' responses. Most of us privilege logic over emotions and instincts. As you enquire about whose truth you've stepped out of, beware of this. Consciously open your heart and attune to your gut feelings. This will require concentrated self-awareness and presence.

Before we begin to look at the practical 'how-to' of discerning our own truth, I want to reference the role of guilt in our decision-making. I've sometimes joked with people that when a woman has a baby the word 'guilty' should be stamped on her forehead because it seems to be such a common experience for most mothers. Guilt can hijack most of us on occasions, especially if we're managing sensitive situations that involve people we care about greatly. So it's vitally important that we learn the difference between appropriate or healthy guilt and inappropriate or neurotic guilt. Appropriate guilt occurs on the cusp of unethical behaviour or directly after it. It's a healthy, functional response to ignoring our own integrity. It provokes us to restore our inner and outer balance through admission of responsibility and making amends. Neurotic guilt, on the other hand, is a learned response to an external demand or to any number of 'orders' we've internalised. David Richo explains it to us in this way:

> Guilt is not a feeling but a belief or judgement. Appropriate guilt is a judgement that is self-confronting and leads to resolution. Neurotic guilt is a judgement that is self-defeating and leads to unproductive pain. Appropriate guilt is resolved in reconciliation and restitution. Neurotic guilt seeks to be resolved through punishment. In appropriate guilt there is accountability. In neurotic guilt there is blame. In short, appropriate guilt is an adult response; neurotic guilt is the response of the scared child within us.[12]

The difference between these two forms of guilt is crucial. One is an authentic response that's rooted in our own sense of what's right and wrong. The other is an imposter that arrived on the back of someone else's belief system. As parents and caregivers who are allies, we carry a great weight of responsibility. We've taken a stand. There isn't anywhere to hide and, as such, we're vulnerable to being misunderstood, unfairly criticised and judged. Given our counter-cultural position, I suggest we may well be susceptible to neurotic guilt too. For myself, learning to differentiate between these two forms of guilt has taken me, repeatedly, to the source of my own wisdom. The bottom line, when it comes to skilling ourselves up to discern truth is this: attention leads to centering. Soak in the experience of what being centred feels like so you're able to recognise it. And keep doing this until you develop a reference point in your body. Then give yourself this gift of connection again and again and again.

---

12   Richo, D. (1991) *How to Be an Adult.* New York, Mahwah: Paulist Press, p.44.

Strategies for discerning our own truth

Consulting with others

You will, I imagine, have heard the phrase 'It takes a village to raise a child.' I'm of the opinion that it equally takes a village to empower the parents and caregivers of gender-expansive children. So find your tribe. When we decide to involve another person in our exploration, we need to choose wisely. I'm not suggesting that you seek out people who only agree with you. I *am* suggesting you turn to people who respect your process and don't try to 'make you wrong' because their creed or opinion must prevail. That's ego dressed up as engagement. Avoid it. When you're seeking to discover whose truth you've stepped out of – your own or someone else's – you need to talk with individuals who understand this as a concept in the first place. In other words, they'll appreciate that one person's map may not be another's. Often, the hallmark of someone who can fulfil this role is their capacity for active listening. Such people listen with all of themselves, and not only a part of their awareness. They won't minimise your concerns or 'tell' you what to do. They will not 'warn' or reproach you. If they ask a question, it's always in a sensitive manner. When someone communicates at this level, silence in the conversation is welcomed as a space for wisdom to emerge into. And if they offer any suggestions, they'll do so in a respectful way. I hope you have such a person in your life already. Unsurprisingly, such people are not readily available to many of us, so we will need to go and look for them. That search may take you to a specialist helpline, a support group or a counsellor. It may motivate you to reconnect with someone you were once close to or to find an inclusive spiritual group. The point is that when we consult with others we make ourselves vulnerable. That, of itself, often leads to priceless insights about our own truth, but only if the person we are confiding in is worthy of our trust.

There's a great deal of value in consulting with other people if we're engaged in active enquiry and the building of self-knowledge.

The simple act of telling your problem to another person can enable you to formulate it clearly. When you hear yourself speaking out loud, sometimes the answer you're seeking is immediately obvious. Or it may be an intuition, question or observation from the person listening to you that will start to unravel the tangle of tension curled up in your belly. In consultation with another there's also the huge benefit of discharging emotion in a 'safe' context if you need to. Then, as you grapple with the 'truth' question, it won't be obscured by unexpressed feeling or dazzled by an overactive mind. If you're not 'secretly' looking for someone to tell you what to do and you limit the number of people you go to for advice, then consulting with carefully selected others can be an invaluable step in 'hearing' yourself into truth.

Consulting with yourself

Keeping company with yourself as you explore this question in depth must be a priority. One of the best ways I know to do this is to develop a relationship with yourself on paper. Journal. As you explore whose truth exactly has been infringed upon, try not to hold back. As far as possible, refrain from censoring yourself – this is critical. Let your feelings lead at this stage. It'll take some practice because most of us write as though we have someone at our shoulder. We're afraid to put down what we really feel in case it's 'wrong' and we'll be punished for it – even when we're sitting alone in our own room. This method of 'stream of consciousness' writing goes some way to undoing this. Persist with it. It'll be useful of itself, and then you can introduce other elements at a later stage.

Put some time and distance between you and the writing and then return to it, switch to a reflective mode and analyse what you find there. Keep on with the detective work. Stay open and listen for your own wisdom. You can also experiment with writing from different perspectives, such as first or second person, or from the perspective of your own inner wise one as you engage in your task. Over several weeks you'll have a lot of material to work with, which you can go through using a highlighter pen to log repeating themes. Feelings of 'guilt' may be one such theme. Are you recognising healthy guilt in your writing or neurotic guilt? And what will you do about it? You may also notice recurring beliefs and associated 'rules' starting to emerge. Does the evidence suggest that they're rigid and outdated or flexible and supportive? And what will you do about it? Or it may be that the paper invites you to simply roam and explore what is right and true for you. This process has served me well and I have a lot of faith in it. I've filled many a notebook, over many decades now, sifting my own truth onto the privacy of the clean, empty page.

Consulting with stillness

To spend time in solitude, silence and stillness, is to prioritise your enquiry. It may feel like a crazy ask to suggest you do this regularly, I get that. Really I do. And…when we're talking about our truth versus someone else's, with all the potential implications this has for our child, it puts the request in a very big context. As allies, we can't afford to scribble 'stillness' at the bottom of our 'to-do' list. We need to make it a priority. I took a long time to learn the value of this, not least because my life was full to bursting and I habitually put other people's needs before my own. Consequently, when I was seriously conflicted, I resorted to my default position of 'paralysis through analysis'. It would hit me like this: first, I'd become preoccupied about the problem I had, and then my mind would embellish it with 'stories' that significantly increased my anxiety; eventually, my self-talk would coil and criss-cross around the same mental circuit so many times I couldn't separate one thought out from another; then I'd grasp at any knot I could reach to undo it, but found it only ever tightened all the others; finally, my mind would go into full-blown overdrive, attempting to sort out the scrape I was in and 'paralysis' would ensue. It was a seriously unhealthy way to function. Gradually, over many years, I found my way to techniques that helped me to 'still' my mind.

I stopped living in my head all of the time and learnt how to centre myself in my body instead. The trio of head, heart and guts finally began to receive equal attention from me. Consequently, I broke through the dominance of rationality in my thinking and stopped limiting myself to logic. All the information that was being held back in my senses began to flood through my self-awareness channels. This holistic approach to conversing with my truth was transformative. I came to recognise that beneath all the mental activity I'd been lost in, a part of me 'knew' the answer I was looking for all along. All I had to do in the end was create the conditions to hear it.

Consulting with courage

When we're seeking to establish whose truth we've stepped out of, we'll spend a lot of time on the edge of our comfort zone. As we journey closer and closer to a conclusion, it may be that we find ourselves travelling away from certainty in other directions. Often this may come about when we assert ourselves differently from the way people want or expect us to. Old patterns of relating get toppled as we speak our newly hewn truth, and this can feel edgy or even, on occasions, explosive. Often it will feel empowering. Ultimately, we must be prepared for all these potentialities, while at the same time aspiring to communicate in healthy ways. Or, we may discover that groups we once aligned ourselves with, now feel strangely at odds with our changing internal reality. And this presents us with a whole set of new possibilities to find our way through. Then again, the journey to truth may have taken us to the door of humility. We step over the threshold and find ourselves apologising, unreservedly, for behaving in ways that are now unacceptable to our growing awareness and self-knowledge. In essence, this depth of inner work will come at a cost. The rewards that follow, in my view, are both abundant and worth it. Above all, we're now qualified, and capable, of asking this question of others. And we might choose to frame it in this way: 'Has my child stepped out of your truth or stepped into their own?'

Withdrawing our allegiance and changing our position is a process. And it's meant to be. What I mean by this is that every stage of a process brings with it a series of potential steps. These steps will present us with choices and decisions to make. Sometimes we have an idea where it's all going and sometimes we don't. As we move through the proceedings, the demands of each stage will test us. Paradoxically, this inner process within the larger one can equip and empower us to manage the very thing we want to overcome. As we confront each obstacle, we have the opportunity to gain resilience, clarity and authority. And this will feed into the next stage of the process, and the next and the next and the next. This is the 'how-to' of building self-belief and agency.

The approach I've been describing above can't do anything else but enrich your self-knowledge, crystalise your self-awareness and authenticate your self-belief. As this takes place, you'll feel increasingly congruent in your life, so what you feel, say and do will match up. This will positively affect your confidence, communication and decision-making capacities. You'll be able to deal with conflict from a more resourceful place and sustain judgemental attitudes with more ease. When you meet professionals, other parents, peers, extended family and community members, it will be from a position of personal strength and innate integrity. This isn't to suggest that you won't ever feel anxious again, or won't have questions or won't feel frightened about the future sometimes. Of course not. As a child-inclusive parent you're in straits most other caregivers or professionals know very little, if anything, about. But you are an ally who has expertise on your child. You have rank because of this. Accept and use the influence it gives you. Your child is depending on it.

We've been giving a great deal of thought about creating the conditions that make changing our position possible:

- acceptance that our outward behaviour is a manifestation of our internalised beliefs about gender
- commitment to the process of change, step by step, aiming for progress over perfection
- recognition that guilt can be healthy and useful, or neurotic and misplaced
- engaging ourselves in practices designed to differentiate our truth from that of others
- establishing the relationship between purpose and intention in our thinking
- accepting our rank as child-inclusive parents and caregivers who have expertise on their child.

Holding all of this in mind and heart, it's time now to build a practical plan of action. You have much within you to draw on to do so now:

- the Four Keys: listening, imagination, empathy and courage
- the Four Ss: self-knowledge, self-awareness, self-forgiveness and self-esteem
- your will-to-do-good
- the work you've undertaken on your gender beliefs and assumptions, which is diminishing your allegiance
- the installation of the principles above, which will enable you to turn around your behaviour.

The 'how to' of changing position

Purpose
Clarity around purpose is essential to successful outcomes. My assumption here is that our purpose is a shared one: *to change our position in relation to the Matrix and protect and accept our gender-expansive children*. You may have heard the phrase 'Energy flows

where attention goes.' In other words, whatever you place your attention on will make it more precise and detailed, and this, in turn, will recruit your energies to it. Our purpose may look like a single athlete standing alone on a running track, but in reality the athlete is part of an extensive team. And it's the combination of skills, strengths and effective relationships around the athlete that make winning the race possible. That's how it is inside our psyches and souls. We have a range of capacities to call on to achieve a purpose that's critical to us, and the will-to-do-good is the manager of the whole roadshow.

Attention–intention–action

This is the simple, galvanising formula that will enable the oil tanker to turn, or the ice shelf to disperse. So let's jump in now. I've no doubt you've been paying a lot of attention to your current position already. You now need to map it out deliberately. To begin this process, allow yourself to 'step back' far enough to feel into everything you've been digesting: the depth of your allegiance to the Matrix, its relationship to your behaviour towards your gender-expansive child, plus where you position yourself in the world at large. Then take a breath. 'The world at large' is a big place. It includes everyone you know and everywhere you go: family, friends, your work setting, place of worship, any learning environment you're in, your neighbourhood, the clubs you go to, the public services you use and the public spaces you visit. I want to remind you of something in capital letters: BECOMING AN ALLY IS A PROCESS, not a one-time event. And please, log again, that we're pursuing progress over perfection. I'm not asking you to take on the whole world at once. I'm only asking that you bring all aspects of your life into view.

When you've spent a good portion of time feeling into how your current position manifests day to day, capture this information in some way: in words, drawings or on a voice-recorder. Be creative. This will never be an exact science. What we're aiming for is a deep felt sense of your position, an inner measurement only you can register.

This might actually translate into figures, such as '70 per cent of the time my allegiance is with my child and my behaviour reflects this', or it might not. The knowing may be more generalised and arrive as a strong 'a-ha' moment, a lancing stab of pain, a tsunami of compassionate empathy for your child, or on a wave of salty hot tears. Remember you have a choice at this juncture. Resort to fight or flight in response to exploring this territory, or stay with your uncertainty and struggle until a new insight is born. If you choose the latter, I guarantee it will happen. Don't forget to take care of yourself as you journey on. The road less travelled is called so for good reason. You're part of a courageous minority of parents and caregivers prepared to do this work, and for that I honour you.

Here are four suggestions to add to your own strategies as you engage with this task. All of them are designed to access information that may be hiding out just below the level of your conscious awareness. I recommend you do them on your own:

- Set yourself questions to answer on paper or on a voice-recorder. Your willingness to do this will pull you more deeply into the current of your own awareness. Have bold questions such as these: 'How far am I prepared to collude with the mainstream to "standardise" my child?' 'Am I looking to my child to rescue me from a baffling or difficult situation?' 'Is my child the scapegoat for adults who won't look at their own "stuff"?' If you're doing this on paper, then write the questions down with your dominant hand, and answer them with your non-dominant hand. Persevere with this. Focus on answering the questions, one by one, before the censor in your mind tries to silence you. Warning: this is a very powerful way to engage with your own truth. Then engage with some of these questions: 'If I could see myself parenting differently, what would it look like?' 'What is it that keeps getting in the way?' 'What does that tell me?' What is it I'm not letting myself know?' 'What would the wise part of me suggest?' 'If I was free of constraints what would I do?' 'What reality do I want to create for me and my child?' 'And what would that mean to me?' You may choose to use the same technique to answer this set of questions, or use 'stream of consciousness' writing instead.

• Another way to illuminate your position is to allow your attention to rest on any key incidents with your child that won't seem to 'let you go'. Choose one. Clear a large space. Identify how many people were involved in the incident and place a corresponding number of mats on the floor. Put an empty chair in the middle of them and imagine your child sitting on it. Then stand in the position you took and recall it in detail. Taking your time, step onto each of the other mats and 'feel into' the position of the person who occupied it. Recall what they said, how they said it and any actions they took. Finally, approach the chair. Imaginatively and empathically, ask your child first how they're feeling. Listen deeply for the answer. Then ask if there's anything you can do that will make a positive difference to their feelings? When this conversation feels complete, explain that you want to change your position and need their help to do so. Ask for their feedback. Then say 'Thank you' and step away from the space. Pause. Return to your original place. Now ask yourself how your perspective has changed and what will you do as a result of this? Then pick up the mats, put the chair back and record the signposting and knowledge you gained about yourself through this process. If you're allowing guilty feelings to inform you, which may be wise, then it's essential to check out whether they're healthy ones or not. Again, remember to show yourself empathy and understanding too, which is a vital component of any challenging inner work we undertake.

- This exercise requires a stack of magazines, two large pieces of card, two pocket-sized pieces of card, scissors and glue. Your task is to create two collages: one that tells the story of where you are now as a parent or caregiver to your child, and the other that tells the story of your future position. Again, work intuitively as far as possible. Let your intention guide your choice of images, even if your conscious mind is confused by your selection. Simply go with your gut. Take your time. When you've finished your 'present' collage, take a break for ten minutes. Make a drink, look out of the window, maybe have a snack. Do not check your phone. Then settle back in and complete the 'future' collage. Place both collages in front of you and look at them in detail, almost as if you've never seen either of them before. Notice the impact each one has on you. Finally, listen for three words inside you that sum up each picture – your present reality and your future one. Write them out on the small pieces of card, one for each collage. Make a decision about how this material can best serve your purpose in an ongoing way.

- Sit quietly and settle your thinking mind. When you've done that, think about your week ahead and what you plan to do in it. Then breathe in gently once or twice and allow yourself to imagine that you personally identify as someone gender-expansive or transgender. Take some time over this. Aim to experience a 'felt' sense of connection to the person you've become. When you've got this, simply walk yourself into your plans for next week: going to work, shopping, having lunch in the park, having a swim, taking the car to the garage, meeting friends, collecting children from school, attending a job interview, visiting a friend's church. Whatever it is, take your 'new' self through each experience in your imagination. Visualise in as much detail as possible, what might occur in each setting. When you've completed the process, take a moment to 'step back into' your real life. Look around the room and take it in; feel both your feet on the ground. Then pick up a pen and paper and jot down your thoughts and feeling about the following: Consider where and when you accrued privileges socially, psychologically and spiritually as you went about your business. Did you feel okay in the changing facilities at the swimming pool? Did the car mechanic treat you courteously? Did the other parents in the playground include you in their conversations? Were you confident you'd been treated equally in the job interview? How welcome were you made to feel at church? On the basis of this, now give some thought to context. How many times in this typical week were you in contexts that conferred high status on you? Or low? Then reflect on how much energy, determination and courage it took to lead your life as a 'normal' person whose gender identity differs from the majority. Finally, take another breath and bring your child into your consciousness. Contemplate their average week, what they might do, who they have to interact with and who they choose to, and consider how much control and influence they have over their time and activities. Jot down everything this brings up for you. Return to the notes soon after and share them with someone you trust.

These activities have the potential to yield a great deal of personal data. All of them can point you in the direction of a desired future. As you pay attention, which means keeping your purpose in mind and heart, begin to plot out a course from one point of learning to another. This is the 'how to' of changing position. In effect, our mantra as allies must now be 'How will I bring my attention, intention and action together?' Here are a couple of examples of the sort of outcomes this exploratory work might yield:

1. *Attention:* Through the process of questioning yourself on paper, you realise that you've been 'caretaking' your child's teacher because they seem willing, though unable, to prevent kids teasing your child. On the back of this you then also realise, with a shock, that this is the emotional equivalent of abandoning your child.

2. *Intention:* You're not going to accept anymore that the school are 'doing their best' when your child is frequently still in tears when you come home from work.

3. *Action:*

    a. You make an appointment to see the class teacher and head teacher.

    b. You ring a specialist helpline and get their advice.

    c. You go into the meeting with a clear outcome in your mind.

    d. You promise your child that you will not leave the meeting until you're fully satisfied with its outcome.

Or:

1. *Attention:* The two collages, side by side, have thrown up some information you've been struggling to come to terms with. Your current position is dictated by fear. The first collage is dominated by 'shadowy' authority figures and you suddenly realise that the perplexing image of a field mouse, curled into a ball, represents both you and your child. You notice that you felt anxious and hopeful completing the second collage, and destroyed them both before your partner came home. This action equally shook you up, as the two of you are close. This has left you wondering if it's to the exclusion of what your gender-expansive child needs?

2. *Intention:* You are going to concentrate on resourcing yourself to become a stronger ally to your child.

3. *Action:*
   a. Retrieve the pieces of collage from the rubbish and put them safely in a clean container.
   b. 'Put an arm around yourself' and ask what it is you need now.
   c. Meet some of that need, if only partially.
   d. Spend 15 minutes 'stream of consciousness' writing, then 15 minutes analysing your feelings.
   e. Identify one new behaviour you'll immediately commit to that supports your child's journey.
   f. Review this material one day later and decide on further intentions and actions.

The dynamic formula of attention–intention–action is the traction you need to both change your position and maintain your progress. Of course, it won't always be plain sailing and it won't happen overnight. Invest for the long term. Revising any behaviour that's habitual, means there will be times when you 'slip up' or even crash-land. The point is to land, and to not disappear emotionally or dig yourself in because you've lost your bearings as an ally. Make the decision to get up and get on with it. And if this feels overwhelming, then put out your hand and borrow the strength of another ally, to help you onto your feet again.

Further techniques for changing position

Change never follows a straight edge. You're well on your way now to dismantling the Matrix inside yourself. As you keep assessing your position and visioning where you want to be with your child, there are techniques and tactics that can support you with this. Here are some that I can recommend to you. No doubt, you'll have others. Behavioural change techniques are far from a new phenomenon, so explore what's available out there and create a favourite catalogue of your own.

S.T.O.P.

A short, sharp signal to yourself, designed to interrupt reactive thoughts or behaviour.

S. Stop.

T. Take a step back.

O. Organise your thoughts and feelings.

P. Proceed.

'Take a step back' might look like a visit to the bathroom, a trip to the car, or 'looking' for your keys. Anything that buys you a few moments to compose yourself, reorganise your internal state and proceed forwards from a more aware-full place.

'Acting as if...'

At its simplest, 'acting as if' means acting as though something were already true for you. When we do this deliberately, we're cooperating with the part of our self that wants to achieve this in reality. As such, we aren't pretending and we're not being inauthentic either. Our will-to-do-good is simply choosing to put aside the limiting beliefs that are still obstructing our highest intentions. We behave as we want to feel. When we 'act as if', we sincerely assume the posture, tone and presentation of someone who's achieved the outcome we want. As we persist with this, a remarkable thing happens. Our feelings and emotions follow suit. Our outer and inner selves join hands. As an ally who is working to undo your own conditioning and to simultaneously support your child, this technique can advance both of these goals quickly.

So, for instance, you may choose to 'act as if' you're fully comfortable with your teen's decision to not identify within the binary. You know how hard they've struggled to fit in and you respect their decision to stand out in this way, and you remain concerned. Plus you don't really 'get' their experience. This adds considerably to your worries and you also feel guilty about these feelings. As a parent or caregiver who is an ally, you've set an intention, in line with your purpose, to support your child's choice. To empower your capacity to achieve this, you practise this technique of 'as if' for several weeks. Over this time, your levels of comfort with your teen's decision start to change and you begin to feel much more relaxed where before you were only anxious. Unsurprisingly, your child is then able to 'relax' into their skin with much more ease, in parallel with you 'acting as if'.

Developing a 'thick skin'

In my experience, developing a thick skin is both a technique and, frequently, an outcome of being an ally. By nature I'm a sensitive person and when I was a lot younger this sometimes felt unmanageable to me. I envied people who seemed to be able to let things 'bounce off' them, with seemingly no after effect. I've had to learn how to respect my sensitivity and, at the same time, not to be engulfed by it emotionally. Gradually I've learnt to 'grow' a thick skin, which I can now 'put on' when I choose to. The equalities and social work I've undertaken over the years have reinforced this know-how. I'm fortunate that I've had enough safety and support in my life to create this as an option. This skill is a result of privilege, not merit. For some people a 'thick skin' means the difference between life and death, though the price they pay for wearing it all the time is costly. Being strong and being tough are not the same. The first includes vulnerability and the second denies it. If we habitually act with a 'thick skin', then eventually our capacity for connection and empathy becomes seriously impaired. This makes for a lonely life. It may also lead to behaviours that damage others. So I'm advocating for the strategic use of this technique, not the blanket use of it. As parents and caregivers we can then act boldly on behalf of our child and still remain highly attuned and sensitive to their changing needs.

As an ally who's committed to protecting and accepting all gender-expansive children, my intention to intervene on their behalf, if necessary, is a given. As such, I will not sacrifice the self-worth of Ruby, or any other child, to caretake a person who cannot receive my feedback as information. If they feel angry or upset because I've called out their behaviour as inappropriate, so be it. My 'thick skin' insulates me from their disapproval. I recognise that it's not my job to pacify their ego, and my 'thick skin' holds me back from caretaking them. My inner wisdom subsequently directs me to my rightful work. My job, as Ruby's grandmother, is to keep her free from harm, as far as possible. And that means physically, emotionally, spiritually and psychologically. As a young child, the foundations of her identity are still being laid down and she's susceptible to every message in her environment about who she is. As I am one of her primary caregivers, she looks to me for approval, guidance and protection. Ruby has extremely limited power and control over anyone or anything. She doesn't need to 'toughen up', she needs to feel safe. My grandchild has to feel confident that if a safety boundary is breached in my presence, I will act decisively. I pray I always will. This might require that I go inwards and drink a draught of courage before I act. Or I may find myself emboldened by Ruby's vulnerability alone. My intention, in either circumstance, is to let my feelings lead, with a level head. And, where I'm able, with an open heart that's seeking accountability, over any need to blame.

Think in a circle

Learning to 'think in a circle' not in a box, which is the cultural norm, is a transformative shift for most of us. A circle has a space for everyone in it, which means there are no corners to shove anyone into. As such, it's a mental tool we can use to monitor our beliefs, bias and prejudice in our daily lives. When we learn to ask ourselves

'Am I thinking in a circle or in a box?', we can differentiate between these things much more speedily.

Thinking in a circle also means that everyone remains in view. Those people we feel comfortable being around and those we don't. Our child lives in a series of concentric circles: family, friends, school, community, culture and society. As we withdraw our allegiance and change our position, we'll begin to survey those circles differently. Our vigilance will increase because our awareness, knowledge and self-belief have. From this viewpoint, we'll be able to 'join up the dots' between a remark made in our child's presence, and the impact it may have on their feelings of self-worth. An event such as this galvanised one young father to take action:

> My uncle was saying things like 'You'd better get him sorted; he's not a girl, he's not a girl' and stuff like that in front of her. He said to my nan but not to my face, 'He's got to get his hair cut.' But I was aware when I went in that there was an undercurrent. I had to say to him, 'You're just going to have to stop referring to my girl as a "he". She is what she is. That's how it is. Either you accept it or we won't come round.' That's difficult isn't it, to know someone in your family feels that way?

The more we learn to think in a circle, the sooner we stop facilitating social niceties to avoid conflict, or go 'off duty' because we've 'lost sight of' our teen. In doing so, the burden of responsibility for our child's welfare rightly stays with us, releasing our kids to get on with the business of growing up healthy, strong and well in themselves. Learn from the past, don't languish there. As the same reflective young father above told me:

> I'll tell you what I've done with work. This was early on when there was a show about transgender people on in the staff room and the debate started around it. I left the staff room 'cause I

didn't want to be exposed and have to confront people, which I
thought would happen. Now I would never do that.

As an ally who is escalating their change of position, the past has
valuable things to teach you. The secret is to not get stuck there. If
you are stuck, then it's possible that you'll begin to get lost in regret,
wallow in self-pity, or do both. Either state will devour your mental
energy if you stay in it too long. The antidote is to feel what you're
feeling fully, which may involve expressing it physically, then to 'let
go of the story' and move into productive action. Agree with yourself
that learning from the event is the way to redeem it, so write it out
stage by stage. Then think about the 'lessons' you've learnt and how to
avoid the same pitfalls that preceded them. This last part is essential.
Absorb the insights, record them, keep them somewhere accessible
and return to them when you need to. None of us can change the past.
We can change our perspective on it though. This simple practice is
one effective way to do so.

Collaboration with your child
Working in alliance, with your child or teen, to accelerate your change
of position can be a great thing to do. But it isn't risk-free, which we
need to consider. As the child-inclusive adult, we need to be wise
about our motivations for collaborating with our kids and clear about
our boundaries. For instance, wanting and needing the approval of
our children can collapse into each other if we're not mindful of this.
If we're constantly checking in to be directed, reassured, advised or
approved of, this will distort the balance of care and responsibility in
the relationship. It will also exhaust our child's energy reserves. This,
in turn, will likely result in them feeling conflicted and probably
resentful. Sadly, the alliance that arose from the promise of change
will then wither from a lack of attention. Obviously, this isn't what
we want. On the other hand, the experience of collaborating with
a child or young person around a shared goal can be a wonderful

thing. Generally, children aren't used to having their knowledge and direct experience validated. Overwhelmingly, their 'voice' is usually absent in any significant decision-making about their needs. So when the opposite happens, and they're recognised as having an investment and expertise, all sorts of benefits may start to blossom. Communication will usually open up and the child's self-esteem will, without question, be enhanced. As they give feedback to us and we receive it as information, confidence and trust will deepen. Accomplishments can be celebrated together. In essence, this healthy model of collaboration is built on clear roles, expectations that have been explicitly agreed upon and the premise that the child is equal, though different, from the adult. It's our full responsibility, as adults, to remain aware of this difference at all times. In doing so, the risk of our needs eclipsing those of our kids is neutralised. Only then are we free to travel, side by side, on our parallel journeys, offering support to each other along the way.

Owning our prejudice

Here is another Google dictionary definition:

> *Prejudice: preconceived opinion that is not based on reason or actual experience.*

Until Ruby's gender journey took us off-piste entirely, I had no idea how much prejudice I'd imbibed to do with gender identity. I had good reason to think I'd covered a lot of ground in this vicinity and could take most things in my stride. Now there's isn't any doubt in my mind that every time I persuaded Ruben out of a skirt and into trousers, or avoided going to public places with him in a dress, I was acting out my prejudice. Beneath my actions was the belief that his behaviour was 'wrong' in some way, and that mine was right. This isn't to say that other, powerfully motivating factors weren't operative in me too; in particular, the need to ensure Ruben would be safe. And this still doesn't discount the other part. The part where prejudice was generating my behaviour to cover up, influence and otherwise talk my grandchild out of expressing his gender the way he wanted to. When I began to recognise this as a truth it was painful to me. I wanted to look away. It was very hard to take full responsibility and say 'no, this isn't right. This isn't right at all.' Like most people, I can talk myself into one corner and then out of another. I can justify my actions and go along with story, even when the niggling feeling just below my breastbone tells me differently. In the early days with Ruben, it was like this more times than I care to remember. In the end though, being disingenuous with him tore at the bonds of trust that wove our hearts together. I came to realise that what kept me awake at night wasn't my grandchild's behaviour, it was my own.

Those of us who recognise we carry prejudice and don't want to, often do a good job of keeping it under wraps and that's commendable. It will eventually leak out though because we're unable to control the 'messages' that our unconscious transmits. The will-to-do-good can guide us, but it's not an invincible force. Here's an example of what I mean by this. Not so long ago I was attending a workshop and I was in the bathroom just before it was due to start. As I was leaving, I held the door open for an elderly woman to pass through. As she hobbled towards me, leaning heavily on a walking stick, I heard my self-talk declare, loud and clear, 'I hope I don't get paired up with her.' I was appalled by this. I know enough about my own prejudice now to catch it by the tail as it retreats back into my psyche, and to hold on to it, to pull it further out and into the light of my awareness, which is what I was able to do on this occasion. I knew then, in that moment, how much ageist thinking I'd internalised and, significantly, how much of my own resistance to the ageing process I was projecting onto the woman who had approached me. If I'd failed to own my prejudice in this situation, several things could have happened over the course of the workshop. I may have been cold towards the woman or avoidant. I might have been over-attentive to compensate for my attitude or I might have patronised her because of it. Or, I could have subdued my guilty feelings all day until I'd rationalised myself out of taking any responsibility for them at all.

There's a lot of fear around talking about prejudice, and defensiveness too. I've lost count of the times people have told me that they're scared of 'saying the wrong thing' and then 'getting into trouble'. And, unfortunately, certain ways organisations and individuals go about addressing this issue justifies their response. It isn't easy territory to spend a lot of time in, and we must develop the stamina to do so. Have you ever had the experience of being present when someone openly confesses to something you know you'd want to hide? Maybe an attitude they have that they don't want, or an action they took that they later regretted? When I witness this sort of raw honesty, it always has a strong impact on me. First, I respect the speaker's willingness to 'show' themselves and be publicly accountable; and second, I realise, again, that lightning doesn't strike when we speak the truth with an open heart.

The majority of us, though, still avoid or hesitate to discuss prejudice if our involvement is implicated in it. Instead we feel guilty for having it and don't quite know what to do except squash these feelings down when they rear their head. Then we're left with the double difficulty of bearing both and actively avoiding this knowledge about our self. Concealment, also uses up a whole lot of mental energy to keep the thing we're ashamed of under lock and key. Sometimes, too, when we allow ourselves to stay 'stuck' in guilt, this is a mechanism fear uses to hold us back from moving forwards. Often, very often, we internally react in a prejudicial way with no conscious intent. It's 'just there', as I've said before. Prejudicial associations often get laid down in our psyches when we're very young. Children are porous and they absorb what's around them without the mature capacity to think critically about it. So there will be times, as adults, when we encounter a difference and will still feel a 'charge' around it, even if we don't understand where it's coming from. The charge registers in our bodies as a response to something 'bad' or threatening in some way. When this happens, we need to talk about it, plain and simple. This is the critical first stage of letting it go. We need to be wise about who we share with, and yet share we must because we can't change a behaviour until we own it. And if we don't own it, it may end up taking ownership of us instead.

How does prejudice escalate?

Gordon Allport, the esteemed psychologist in post-war 1950s America, was tasked with identifying the stages that preceded the Jewish Holocaust and the systematic murder of marginalised groups in World War II. His model, known as Allport's 'Ladder of Acting out Prejudice', looks like this:

- **Rung 1 – Speech:** This is where it starts. When speech – meaning 'jokes', insults, rumours, degrading names, written material, stereotypes and gossip – all conspire to mark the targeted group as 'wrong' and 'all the same'. If this goes unchallenged, then 'safe spaces' are established that allow such speech to become normalised and unquestioned. Essentially, camaraderie is slyly embedded on the basis of projecting hate onto the same figures.
- **Rung 2 – Avoidance:** On this level, people actively avoid being close to, or associating with, the group that has been stereotyped. This means refusing to use the same shops, leisure facilities, places of worship or businesses. It means forbidding one's children to make friends with a child from this group, or challenging the school system to prioritise your child's needs over the child from the outcast group. The dangerous thing about such self-imposed isolation is that it leads to greater ignorance. If there's no contact, there's no hope of friendship.

And friendship humanises the other. No friendship means pervasive ignorance and 'social blindness' as to the real conditions of another person's life. This then breeds fear and the solidifying of prejudice into direct action.

- **Rung 3 – Discrimination:** And here's where it gets explicit, if we have eyes to see. This is when direct or indirect action is taken against a group, or any one person in it. Either way, the victim is reduced only to their difference. Here's how one person describes this: 'When we are discriminated against, whatever the multi-layered experience we may have of our own identity in life, we know we are part of that group. This is the fist-in-the-face moment.'[13]

  Discrimination includes being excluded from social clubs, churches, institutions and workplaces. It includes the deliberate withholding of knowledge so that success in any endeavour is sabotaged. Discrimination includes being denied basic rights, such as housing, healthcare and education, or being forced out of the community you once called home. When laws are enacted from this rung of the ladder the consequences are chilling. Effectively these laws make it legal for *society* to discriminate.[14]

- **Rung 4 – Subtle Aggression:** This is all about entitlement. If someone's positioned here, they believe in a hierarchy of power that's both inalienable and based on 'deficit' assumptions about

---

13 Fanshawe, S. and Sriskandarajah, D. (2010) 'You can't put me in a box: Super-diversity and the end of identity politics in Britain.' Institute for Public Policy Research (IPPR), p.8. Available at www.ippr.org/publications/you-cant-put-me-in-a-box-super-diversity-and-the-end-of-identity-politics-in-britain, accessed on 14 July 2017.

14 The UK Immigration Act 2014 now requires private sector landlords to check the immigration status of their tenants. This is controversial legislation, not least because it recruits landlords to do the work of border control and financially penalises them if they fail to do so. Human rights lawyers also believe that it legitimises bias and potentially provides a smokescreen for the enactment of prejudice and discrimination.

targeted groups. These negative assumptions are consistently communicated in multiple subtle ways, which include hostile 'looks', silences, withholding courtesies and persistent, deliberate use of high-rank signals. These 'micro-aggressions' are intended to psychologically diminish the person they're being directed at.

- **Rung 5 – Physical Attack:** Physical attack of people or property takes many forms. It may be a brick through the window, or a twisted newspaper set on fire and pushed through a letter box. It may be the defacing of graves, graffiti on a door or any other action designed to terrorise and intimidate. But at this level of the ladder, none of the above may satisfy the perpetrator. Drawing blood may be the only thing that satiates the hatred this person projects onto another.
- **Rung 6 – Extermination:** We have reached the top of Allport's Ladder. From here the persecutor is elevated and can see no other perspective except their own. This final, dreadful step sees an acceleration from murder to genocide – the systemic attempt to destroy an entire people. The consequences of this will scar, shape and burden generations to come.

Prejudice is never a private matter. It *always* requires a recipient. It doesn't exist without one. And prejudice is the king pin in the cycle of oppression that gets acted out daily in situations around us. As we've seen, in the beginning, there's a difference, which gets stigmatised in all or some of the ways we've been looking at in this book. Someone's religion, their skin colour, their nationality, their gender identity or their sexual orientation will be cast as abhorrent or inferior in some way. This then gets generalised to encompass a whole group.[15] Suddenly, it switches from being a specific person someone 'has a

---

15   If an individual belongs to several targeted groups at once, then their multiple identities 'intersect' to make a whole that is different from its individual parts. Their vulnerability to prejudice and discrimination increases accordingly.

problem with' and starts being the entire group the person is part of. The 'you' becomes the 'they', the singular becomes 'that lot'. Once more, we're squarely into the territory of in-group/out-group identity. When we see in stereotypes, we speak in stereotypical terms. If these generalisations are reinforced by society at large, by our education system, economic institutions, faith centres, the judiciary, policy-makers and the media, then essentially all evidence to the contrary will be filtered out of our awareness. The prejudice will gain credence and acceptability, and even kudos. And when these dynamics are exploited by political stakeholders, who cynically use these divisions to propagate fear and prop up their position, then we've entered very dangerous territory indeed. As Voltaire, the eminent French philosopher, warned us over 300 years ago, 'Those who can make you believe absurdities can make you commit atrocities.'[16] Gordon Allport's Ladder shows us how.[17]

I've got it, so how do I rid of it?

I'm of the view that we can never eradicate our own prejudice fully. We can stop being afraid of it though, and we can dig into it and pull out its roots whenever we come across them. The work you've been doing as you've progressed through this book will have reduced your bias and prejudice already, as surely as sunshine burns through fog. The exercises and reflections that follow will do the same.

Self-talk

Our self-talk, again, is the entrance to insight and growing self-awareness and knowledge. This time, it will lead us straight to our prejudice if we allow ourselves to be taken there. Do you recall the story I told about the older woman walking past me into the bathroom? When I 'heard' myself say that I hoped she wouldn't be

---

16   Available at www.brainyquote.com/citation/quotes/quotes/v/voltaire118641.html, accessed on 07 September 2017.

17   Clements, P. and Spinks, T. (2006) *The Equal Opportunities Handbook*, 4th Edition. London and Philadelphia: Kogan Page. pp.16, 29–30.

in my workshop, I realised that thought existed in a context. I knew that sitting beneath it would be all sorts of assumptions I wasn't conscious of. Not least that, as an older person, the woman would be 'slow' in her thought processes and might slow up my process too. What was my evidence for assuming this? The older person I've stood behind in a shop queue while she struggled to find her coins? The older man who took forever to fill his car with petrol as I impatiently waited behind him? Or my Aunty Iris, who at 87, taught herself to use a computer to correspond with her friends around the world? Then learnt how to take pictures on her mobile phone so she could send them along with her lengthy, engaging and witty emails. Given this intimate example of inspirational older age, why did my brain opt for the default stereotype of an older person who wouldn't be quick-thinking or interesting anymore? Because that's the dominant one I've absorbed from our ageist culture. Happily, in this instance, I 'caught' my self-talk and was able to own it, locate its origin, and reflect on how to dispense with it. Over the course of researching and writing this book, I've had a lot more reason to practise this process too. My self-talk has directed me to other forms of bias and prejudice I carry, often in understated and indirect disguise.

It's been my privilege now to have met a number of transgender people, who've been supportive of my work. Usually we've talked together in a café or office space and, at least initially, my self-talk often sounded something like this:

> *I wouldn't have guessed. Keep making eye contact. I can't tell at all. His voice is too gentle. Stop thinking these thoughts. Her voice is a bit deep. Use the right pronoun. It must be so hard. I really can't tell. I wonder if they've got a partner? Make sure you don't stare. Her make-up looks good. His clothes look a bit baggy. For goodness sake, Anna! Just concentrate on the person. Concentrate on the person. Concentrate on the person...*

Even now as I share this with you, I feel some shame about these thoughts. It's never my intention to objectify someone or to treat their lived experience as something I can pick over until I'm satisfied it's genuine. But my self-awareness pointed to a part of me that was doing exactly this. As I acknowledged this fact, over the weeks and months these agitated internal monologues began to cease. They did so, I believe, because I accepted the reality of where I was positioned, so had no need to defend my ego against it. When I've spoken about this with other people, they frequently want to reassure me that my responses were simply a 'natural' reaction to a difference I'm not familiar with. That may be so, and I know full well that mixed in with unfamiliarity is a good dose of prejudice, myth and misinformation that, as a cisgender person, I've picked up over a lifetime. These are the ingredients I have to work with. If I resist owning the prejudice I'm carrying, I'm not only perpetuating it, I'm promoting it. This is hard medicine to take, yet the cure is worth it.

Talk to someone who will be accepting and non-judgemental

An interpersonal context is usually the best environment to change our interpersonal beliefs and behaviours. As I've said before, very often it's only when we hear ourselves speak that we know what we're actually thinking, which is why openly sharing our thoughts is so important. This has been an immensely important aspect of my own journey, some of which I've taken in therapy. A sense of shame diminishes when we say the thing we've concealed out loud and remain accepted by the person listening to us. Then a space opens up to explore all the corners of it, and to coax out all the fears that are crouching there. A supportive person can offer insights, help to unpick our beliefs and embed new learning. They may also disclose their own experiences of acting out prejudice. We learn that we're only human after all. Sharing 'out loud' releases us from the grip of neurotic guilt and it also releases others from the same. When we express our vulnerability in this way, we're also expressing strength of character. In this context, we're able to gradually 'hear ourselves' lovingly accepting the child our prejudice has been obscuring until now.

Thought-stopping

One way to influence our self-talk and begin to uproot automatic prejudice is to practise thought-stopping.[18] This is a simple, though challenging process that has to be persevered with over time to be effective. It works like this. Think about a specific prejudice that you carry, then choose a positive mental image or statement, then create a relationship between the two; in other words, when you notice a stereotypical thought arising, or prejudice surfacing, interrupt this dynamic sharply with the image or statement. While this might feel artificial or superficial to some people, thought-stopping is a powerful technique we use in our everyday lives – we just don't call it that. For instance, imagine you're sitting on a packed plane and it's almost time for take-off. The captain's told the cabin crew to 'take their places' and the lights have been dimmed. Now imagine you could take a reading of the sum total of passengers' thoughts in the cabin. What percentage, might you guess, were practising thought-stopping as a way to manage their anxiety about flying? A considerable number, I think (and I'd be one of them). Thought-stopping is useful and functional when we harness it intentionally to counter any sort of negativity. Prejudicial thoughts and feelings are no exception. Gradually, the positive image or statement you've chosen will begin to weaken your automatic response and, in doing so, free you up to generate a new one based, this time, on your own agency, intelligent thinking and the will-to-do-good.

Strengthen yourself to strengthen others

This might seem like an odd direction to take in relation to routing our prejudice. Why would strengthening our self-esteem impact on the prejudice we carry? The simple fact is that when we feel good about ourselves we have less need to scapegoat other people,

---

18   Thought-stopping is not to be mistaken with the psychological defence of repression. The first is a deliberate strategy to counter material you're fully conscious of. The second is a way to keep this material out of your conscious awareness at all costs.

to project our discontent, fear and feelings of inadequacy onto an out-group person. We're not invested in making someone else 'small' so that we can feel 'big'. Consequently, we don't easily get sucked into unhealthy group behaviours and our reputation is enhanced because of this. The bottom line is clear: the greater our personal sense of security, the less threatened we are by people who are different to us, and the more liberty we have to express ourselves unselfconsciously. I witnessed a lovely example of this only a few nights ago. My youngest son, Leo, was celebrating his 30th birthday and he'd arranged a big party. As the evening went on and more of his friends arrived from far and wide, I noticed a striking similarity between how they all greeted him. The young men all threw their arms around my son, many of them kissed him, held onto him and squeezed his neck. They were completely liberated in their expression of friendship and felt no need to apologise for their love. Because of this, there was also no need to make any quips about 'being gay' to cloak embarrassment in. Later on, several of Leo's friends, who are now fathers, took the time to ask me for advice about childrearing, which was very touching.[19] Leo's friends openly expressing their affection, and these young fathers expressing their need for guidance, are absolutely connected for me. Because the climate in my son's friendship group is one where men support each other and are, to a greater and lesser extent, open about their emotions, this has released them to be more emotionally available in their roles as fathers. Not only this, but these young men have not fallen foul of a pervasive trap the Matrix sets up culturally. They know that masculinity doesn't depend on sexual orientation. Consequently, they feel free to express their love for each other, irrespective of this. In strengthening themselves, they're able to strengthen others.

---

19   There's increasing evidence accruing now that changing norms around childcare has the potential to 'undo' fixed gender roles, and emotionally benefit men in particular. See: Allen, J. 'Changing roles for transforming gender.' *Engenderings* blog from London School of Economics. Available at http://blogs.lse.ac.uk/gender/2016/11/07/changing-parenting-roles-for-transforming-gender, accessed on 23 July 2017.

Choosing to challenge prejudice

Our children are subject to prejudice under the dictatorship of the Gender Matrix. And that prejudice can be located in any one of the concentric circles that surround them: the inner circle of family, the following one of friends and acquaintances, the next circle of neighbourhood and community, the wider circle of the environment we're living in and the overarching cultural circle our lives are infused with. Any, or all of these places, may harbour prejudice towards our child. This can feel like a frightening prospect, and for good reason. Equipping yourself to identify, target and confront prejudice is a way to actively reduce parental fear. The more capable you are of doing this for yourself, the more confident you'll be to address it in someone else.

Susanne is a well-spoken, assertive and energetic older woman who home-schooled her first grandchild, Kat, for six months. Kat's mother is white British and her father, black British. During this period, Susanne and Kat discovered a shared love of language, and of Shakespeare, in particular:

> We'd gone up to see *Othello* in London. I was with Paul, my husband, who had also got into Shakespeare with us. This was before Kat had come out as being transgender. Her hair was short and she was quite androgynous in her appearance. She was about 14 then. I was stroking the back of her neck and watching the performance. We were just sitting there, and Paul was just sitting forward, and there was a couple sitting behind us and there was a black woman sitting on the other side of Kat. Then the couple sitting behind us said at half-time, 'Excuse me I just want you to know that you've absolutely ruined this performance for us, and that boy, that boy, you know, what's he doing wriggling around all the time?' They were just horrible. Kat is the most polite and sweetest person, who's never offensive at all, and she said, 'Would it be better if I sat on the floor?' and I said, 'No, you

just stay where you are,' and the woman on the other side said, 'He's been fine, what are you talking about?' I refused to move. Another couple further along saw this and said, 'Why don't you swap places with us?' The couple behind said we should, and I said, 'We are not going to move. Those people that have offered to swap, I suggest you do.' I wasn't going to let it pass. The other woman was lovely. Paul couldn't cope, he got up and left and missed the second half. Kat and I sat there and watched the second half and enjoyed the whole thing, but after that I realised what had offended this couple sitting behind us. It was the fact that I was sitting stroking the back of a teenage 'boy's' neck, because I'd said, 'Anyway she's a girl.' I was smoothing Kat's neck because she had serious problem with itchy eczema and I knew it helped her to feel calm and concentrate better. I realised that if Kat had been a boy I would've been a bit more self-conscious. With a girl you can do that and think nothing of it, but with a boy you might feel a bit more self-conscious. I thought, 'Mind your own business.' I realised afterwards that they might have been wondering what a black child was doing in the theatre with a white woman and I said, 'Actually she's a girl,' because I wanted to shake them up about their other assumptions too.

When you challenge another person about their prejudice, directly or indirectly, they will rarely appreciate it. Generally, if you do so with respect, upholding their dignity and safety, as well as your own, then it's highly unlikely any conflict will escalate. Occasionally someone will thank you and that will be a beautiful surprise. Perhaps that person may even be one of us in some future circumstance. I hope so. Mostly though, in the first instance, the majority of people may balk at being challenged, even when it's delivered skilfully and with care. We must get used to this and rely on our 'thick skin', in some circumstances, to get us through, as Susanne did above. Despite the very public nature of the confrontation she was involved in, which in the United Kingdom is culturally uncomfortable, to say the least, she refused to back down. Susanne believed the couple's twofold assumptions about Kat exposed their prejudice and positioning hidden behind a curtain of 'civility'. In other situations, the challenge may lead to a courageous conversation and one that will remain with the other person long after we've left them. As allies, we must be willing to do the heavy work of detoxifying the circles our kids move in, especially when we factor in the influence of adult power. Learning how to do this will take time, and for some of us the process will be easier than for others. The formula is the same though: pay attention to what's going on around you, set an intention to intervene if your child's well-being is threatened, then act to protect them. Our expertise or ease in this, or even how the other person responds to us, doesn't matter. What does matter is that our children know we will come to their defence, and do so with agency and vigour.

CHAPTER 10

TURNING OUTWARDS

Spending time with difference

The survival of the Matrix depends on people remaining separated by their gender differences and alienated from each other. As we continue to dismantle it in our thoughts and our behaviour, one sure-fire way of accelerating this process is to spend time with folk who are not 'like me', yet so few of us consciously choose to do this. I had an unlikely experience, many years ago, that got me wondering about this in depth. I was camping in a remote spot on the wild mountains that stand guard over the Welsh coast and the Irish Sea. I hadn't seen anyone for a day or so. The weather was moody and I peeked out of my tent to see if there was any hope of it changing. I saw two things in my line of sight as I looked: a horizon where clouds were being thrown around like soft toys, and a person moving steadily several hundred yards away from me. Various thoughts struck me in that moment: Is this what it was like when indigenous people observed a stranger approaching the land they lived on? At what point did their difference become a threat? When, indeed, does someone who is not 'like me' become someone I treat like an enemy?

When we confine ourselves to specific groups, when we become habituated to everything in our lives, when we avoid people who aren't 'like us', we're setting up a dynamic that makes engaging with difference very hard. We begin to occupy an echo chamber of our own opinion. If we only ever exist in the middle of it, then experiencing life on any edge at all can start to feel dangerous. Consequently, we run the risk of projecting our fears outwards. One of the best ways to rid ourselves of prejudice and bias towards any person or group we relate to negatively is to associate with them. To coin a well-used phrase: 'It's not rocket science.' It's obvious that when we increase our contact with people we've been aloof from, it humanises them. If we're serious about breaking down our bias and prejudice, the chances are we'll realise that many of our perceptions are, in fact, misconceptions. And the same may be true for them about us. So how can we get to spend time with folk who are different from us? There are multiple ways, both literal and virtual.

I didn't go to university until I was in my late 30s, and it was here I discovered the work of Audre Lorde. Her writing had an immediate and profound impact on me. The world lost a pillar of integrity and a temple of courage when she passed away, too soon. Lorde was a self-identified Black, Lesbian, Feminist, Warrior, Poet. She did not look like, sound like or behave like anyone I had ever known. We didn't hail from the same people or even live in the same country. Yet Lorde's essays and poems took me across the tracks to places I had little, if any, knowledge of. Through engaging with her teachings, which meant resisting the impulse to say 'No, this has nothing to do with me', my inner landscape as a white, heterosexual, educated woman changed, and consequently who I was in the world eventually changed too. There are other authors, poets, artists and academics I could point to who have enabled me to spend time with difference. In any given day we can watch a programme, listen to a podcast, read a pamphlet, devour a book chapter, have a powerful conversation or visit an exhibition that will extend our awareness and challenge our prejudice. I want to state the obvious: exposure to difference isn't actually the problem here. It's our willingness to interact with difference that's the real issue. This amounts to the willingness to witness the lived experience of another person who isn't 'like me', to truly put to one side our opinions, objections and entitlement, in an effort to expand our personal consciousness and humanise the stranger-enemy in our view.

One of the finest ways we might be privileged to accomplish this is by opening ourselves up to personal testimony. The truth of this came home to me, significantly, one year when I was struggling to effect change in a national transport organisation I was working with. Despite my best attempts, many participants in the groups I ran felt bewildered and besieged by the cultural shift towards more inclusive work practices. This resulted in high levels of defensive behaviour, which, ultimately, served no-one. Finally I realised that all the theories, statistics, policies and procedures represented a story that had little substance to most people I was working with. I saw that the story that needed to be told had to be from the perspective of a main character, and not a bystander who was, effectively, commentating from a distance. This led me to invite people from non-mainstream groups within the organisation to tell their stories to the local groups I was running. The impact was spellbinding. I remember one occasion in particular, when Steve, a gay man, came to speak with us. I'd been put in touch with Steve via another colleague and I knew nothing of his story. I was concerned about this, but Steve reassured me he would be 'absolutely fine'. I respected his view but started the session with a sense of unease. First, Steve spoke about the loyalty he had to the company he'd been part of for 20 years; and how impossible it felt to disclose his sexual orientation because of the implicit and explicit homophobia he witnessed at work. He talked about how this created a split in him that was exhausting to maintain and seemed impossible to bridge. On the one hand, Steve's 'secret' ensured his safety in the organisation and, on the other, it meant he felt as though he was 'living a lie'. As he shared more and more, his audience listened intently. This emotional 'call and response' dynamic generated its own momentum and I began to feel increasingly anxious. Another 15 minutes or so and I was on the edge of my seat, willing Steve to be quiet. He wasn't, and what followed galvanised everyone in the room. Steve recounted how he'd once been in a long-term relationship and how he and his partner had agreed on a trial separation. Three days later, this man whom he still loved deeply, was killed in a motorbike collision. Steve went into work, day after day, silently reeling from shock and devastating grief. If it had been his wife or girlfriend, he told us, he could have depended on sustained support from his colleagues. Given that it was his boyfriend, he was too broken to risk any sort of rejection. Several months after this tragedy in his life, someone at work 'outed' Steve. What followed brought him close to a complete breakdown. Several of his so-called good friends abandoned him, others bullied and harassed him, and two senior managers attempted to stymie his career. The strength, character and determination it took to survive the experiences Steve suffered were self-evident to all of us in the room that day. As he finished sharing his story, the stereotypes about gay men being 'weak', faithless in love and inadequate in life lay in shreds at Steve's feet.

People in the group were changed through listening to this story. As they stood in a queue to shake hands with Steve at the end of the session, mine stopped trembling. This generous man, who'd given an hour of his life to tell his story with no guarantee of acceptance, had not been reduced to one aspect of his identity. The group had been given the opportunity to spend time with difference and they'd accepted it. Steve had talked from his heart, they had responded from theirs and bridges had been both built and crossed in the time we were together. Stories, above all else, have the power to transform us if we're prepared to listen to them.

I never imagined when Ruby invited me to step into her story as an ally that my decision to do so would lead me to this point. I never imagined that my 'yes' to her, would mean a 'yes' to so many other people too. My life is infinitely richer because of this. I've been privileged now to meet several gender-expansive children, to consult with transgender youth and transgender women and men, and to watch Ruby snuggling up with another child, just like her, when our two extended families spent time together. Significantly, I've met other allies who've also been chiselling at the rock face of the Matrix, long before I knew it even existed. I can guarantee that your decision to reject the gender binary and breathe in the fresh air of diversity will bring you riches too. You'll discover yourself in conversations you never imagined you could have, with people you never imagined you could be friends with. Or you'll find yourself being invited to events and gatherings you never knew existed. It'll be fun as well as unfamiliar, I promise you. The more able you are to listen and learn from others, the more your own reality will be mirrored back as partial. A deep awareness of this will birth greater acceptance, insight and empathy in you. Ultimately, as allies to gender-expansive children, when we spend time with this difference the world will change for us – it will feel larger, more colourful and fascinating as a result of this decision.

Opening up to community

As the parent or caregiver of a gender-expansive child, you have the passport to become part of a remarkable community. The big picture is that the global gender-busting community is multifaceted, complicated, diverse, gritty, resilient, turbulent and dynamic. It isn't 'tidy' and, most definitely, can't be put into any sort of box. I've experienced my brain spinning on a thread as I've attempted to make sense of it, not least because I'm a visitor rather than a native of this land. Yet I also recognise that on another level this tribe is made up of 'ordinary' people who are getting on with their ordinary lives: paying the rent, sorting out relationships, tackling emails, dreaming of change, making sure there's enough washing powder left. I find it both daunting, and reassuring to know that Ruby, her parents and I have this clan at our back: daunting, because it's mostly a mystery to me; and reassuring, because I know it's vibrant, visible and available to my growing granddaughter. For me, turning outwards and into the world has meant opening up to this community. It's meant naming myself not only as an ally but as an activist too.

Contributing to community

People can sometimes feel anxious when they hear the term 'activist'. It's another one of those words that conjure up all sorts of images and assumptions we might want to distance ourselves from. For me, its definition is a simple one: activism is where my inner journey and the outer world meet. In other words, my behaviour on the outside is a reflection of my journey, as an ally, on the inside. So it isn't a fixed thing – my life as an ally changes and develops as I do.

There are many ways to express activism and, as ever, those ways will be as creative and varied as we are. There isn't a test to pass or an exam to sit that confers this badge on us. We don't need to wear a tee-shirt advertising our allegiance to gender diversity or feel driven to give talks or attend protests about gender inclusivity. However, we may want to do each one of those things. In fact, many parents and caregivers on this journey have found themselves to be spokespersons for the rights of LGBTQ kids, even though they never expected to be.[1] When we break open our concept of gender, other ideas about who we can and can't be may break open too.

Our activism counts wherever we commit to demonstrating it. Charities and organisations that serve children like ours have very little financial support other than donations. So this is an easy win for us as allies. Alternatively, if you're living on a low income and have some free time, you can fundraise. Not only will you generate money you're unable to personally give, fundraising creates new connections

---

1   Wayne Maines is one such father. I recommend his deeply personal TED talk: 'Facing Our Fears Can Change the World', available at www.youtube.com/ watch?v=5tzEpqDtaPE, accessed on 27 July 2017.

and builds community of itself. And, if you contact organisations directly about the specific needs they have, you may soon find yourself volunteering admin time to an LGBTQ organisation that's overloaded, or lobbying government for policy changes, or using social media to highlight the challenges gender-expansive children face.

The opportunity for activism is always close and our self-awareness will alert us to this. I was recently at an event in a corporate setting. I was aware that I had a whole bag of assumptions about 'them' in my head, clamouring for freedom, before I'd even taken my seat! I was thinking from inside the box, not from within the circle. The time came for everyone to introduce themselves and briefly say something about their work. As each person took their turn and it got closer and closer to mine, I was deciding on what to reveal. Should I mention I was writing a book? Should I disclose what it was about? What would 'these people' think if I did so? Would it be awkward afterwards? Were any of my tribe in the room? The man next to me finished talking about his role as a senior manager. He glanced sideways and smiled at me as all eyes focused in my direction. I took a breath. Then I walked away from all the unfounded beliefs and strategic thinking in my head, centred in my body and made a decision: yes, I would take this opportunity to be visible, to nail my colours to the mast, irrespective of whether anyone joined in with me or not. In this context, the worst thing that could happen would be that I'd end up eating lunch alone. It probably doesn't surprise you that I didn't. In fact, I ended up having several interactions with different people who were curious and open about gender identity in children. These conversations, which challenged my bias beautifully, also gave me another opportunity: to practise naming myself as an ally in an environment I'm not entirely at ease in. And naming, as you know, brings something alive. So I used the following opening statements several times: 'As an ally to gender-expansive children...' or, 'As an ally to gender-diverse people...' Each time I did so, the weight of the words grounded me in my own truth, and my courage, confidence and conviction followed. When we're in a group, we never know what histories and stories walk into a room with each person. I'm always glad to be reminded of this. Much later on that day, I was working in a pair with another participant at the event. The person I'd been partnered up with had overheard our discussion around the lunch table and it had impacted strongly on him:

> My daughter's gender non-conforming, which has always been problematic for my wife and I. Just recently we clashed with her, and she accused me of being ashamed of her. I denied it. But listening to your conversation at lunchtime, made me realise that it's true.

The benefits of community

When I think of community, I don't imagine shared pot-luck suppers or street parties, a specific neighbourhood group or a location that you need a pass to get into it. Community, to me, is characterised by commitment. Collectively, this commitment is best recognised by its outcome – it creates a certain sort of home for its people, a place to go out from and return to, as it were. One hopes that it's a place of safety where gifts can be shared, sadness accepted and the ordinariness of everyday life appreciated, even if, as so often is the case now, that place is never contained within a physical space. In recent times, a rainbow of genders has been made visible and accessible through technology in a way that was unimaginable to previous generations. As a result, the debilitating isolation and alienation that many gender-diverse people survived, or not, have now been massively reduced for our young people,[2] for which I am truly grateful. But we are still far away from celebrating safety. Because of this, access to, and

---

2   Diane Ehrensaft, in *The Gender Creative Child*, includes a very useful section on the impact of social media on the lives, and the identities, of our gender-expansive kids: Ehrensaft, D. (2016) *The Gender Creative Child: Pathways for Nurturing and Supporting Children Who Live Outside Gender Boxes.* New York, NY: The Experiment LLC, pp.230–7.

membership in, community remains a fundamental survival strategy for many. However much involvement we choose, according to our varied experience and needs, contact with others who can empathise with our situation can rarely be substituted.

Belonging

Belonging is when we 'find each other'. It's when we recognise in someone else a shared understanding based on a similar experience. The feelings this gives rise to are intangible and unmistakable. For us as parents or caregivers this is important. Belonging to a community provides a place to share our story with others, to have a heart-to-heart or to laugh together until our bellies ache. Sometimes eye contact alone will be sufficient to convey that someone understands where we're at. For our children, though, belonging in a community might be lifesaving. Our kids frequently find themselves in situations where they feel 'different', and while this can be a novelty, it's one that's unlikely to last over the long term. Psychologists, researchers, artists and activists confirm that a positive sense of belonging impacts favourably on mental health, emotional well-being, confidence and quality of life. 'Hanging out' with other kids – simply *being kids* together – reinforces sameness, which may be a rare commodity in the lives of our children. Being stigmatised won't necessarily, of itself, erode their self-esteem, but the opportunity to mix with others who are similarly stigmatised will definitely safeguard it.[3]

Courage

I've spoken a lot about courage in this book. Courage is found by sitting in the fire. We don't know if we possess it until we're required to prove it. As I write these words, the iconic image of the Chinese

---

3   GATE Civil Society Expert Working Group (2013) *Critique and Alternative Proposal to the 'Gender Incongruence of Childhood' Category in ICD-11*. Buenos Aires, April 4–6, 2013, footnote 21. Available at https://globaltransaction.files.wordpress.com/2012/03/critique-and-alternative-proposal-to-the-_gender-incongruence-of-childhood_-category-in-icd-11.pdf, accessed on 14 July 2017.

student standing with his arms by his side, in the path of an oncoming tank in Tiananmen Square in 1989, flashes into my mind. I am in awe of every parent and caregiver who, like this unnamed hero, refuses to kowtow to a system hell-bent on contorting their child into its image. Some people can be extraordinary role models for us, whether we share their difference or not. I'm thinking now of a close friend of mine, a young lesbian woman who works with survivors of violence. As a child, she was subject to the sort of abuse that stained even the farthest hem of her innocence. The courage she has found, over and over again, to create self-worth and meaning in her life, never, ever, ceases to inspire me. Whenever I'm afraid to do the thing I need to do, I look to my friend as a reference point. I need to model my own courage on people who exemplify it. And, for good reason, as Frances Moore Lappé articulates: 'Appreciating that community is essential to human well-being calls us to a particular kind of courage: walking with our fear of exclusion in order to stand up for inclusion.'[4]

Solidarity

To experience solidarity with others is a psychological super-boost. It translates as unity around a shared purpose, a guarantee of support and direct action if need be. At best, it means we can depend on other people covering our back, on resources being made available to us, and on allies working to empower us and our loved ones. It equates to a measure of peace, because solidarity in community means that as parents and caregivers we can act collectively from a position of strength. LGBTQ rights, at this particular moment in the United States, are again fiercely under attack and susceptible to being traded for political gain. Where there's solidarity in community, someone is always on watch – day in, day out, 24/7. We don't have to do it all by

---

4   Zamor, R. C. (2017) What Is Community, and Why Is It Important? Available at www.ikedacenter.org/thinkers-themes/themes/community/what-is-community-responses, accessed on 14 July 2017.

ourselves. The Internet may be responsible for much that undermines our cause, but, happily, it's also responsible for much that unites, protects, excites and progresses it. The dirty work of oppression continues, though concealing it has never been more difficult.

Hope

Community can enable us to stay connected to hope. As allies, one resource we need a lot of is optimism. Some days it can feel in short supply. At times like these, supportive contact with another person may be all that it takes to ignite the flame again. And when we feel hopeful today, we feel more able to deal with the possibility of difficulties tomorrow. Make no mistake: hope isn't the quiet neighbour of a more exalted quality, such as courage. Hope is a transfusion that can flood us with the will to act and the life force to achieve it. Community embodies both the act of hope and a refusal to be denied what's being hoped for. The historian and journalist, Rebecca Solnit, pierces the propaganda and pessimism that attempts to quell it. She tells us:

> Your opponents would love you to believe that it's hopeless, that you have no power, that there's no reason to act, and that you can't win. Hope is a gift you don't have to surrender, a power you don't have to throw away.[5]

Celebration

We should never wait to celebrate. Joy is a precious commodity and when it arrives we must jump up and welcome it. To celebrate something as part of a community is an ancient tradition, which often initiates someone into a new phase of their life. Today, mainstream rituals include marriage, being received into faith-based groups

---

5   Solnit, R. (2016) *Hope in the Dark: Untold Histories, Wild Possibilities*. Edinburgh: Canongate, p.xi.

and baby showers. These events validate and affirm the choices that people are making in their lives. Communities who are marginalised must initiate themselves and there's a long and rich history of them doing so. Our children have the right to have their gender-journey milestones recognised, respected and celebrated too. And a close, inclusive community will provide the context for this to happen.

Creating community

A few years ago I met a woman who had lived in an 'intentional' community – one that was built around shared ideals and principles – for eight years. We were chatting away about her time there and I brightly remarked how fortunate I was to live in a city of half a million people, yet not feel isolated at all. I remember that she paused, for just the slightest moment, before she looked into my face and said, 'Anna, some people live in community because they need it, and other people live in community because they know how to create it.' Her insight felt like a gentle rebuke and one I later reflected on in depth. I recall walking by her side and thinking, 'Oh, it's not all about me then.' Indeed it isn't. Community doesn't exist in a vacuum, and everything it offers is dependent on what's being contributed to it. We all have something to bring to its shared table, and we can all take something away from it too. As parents and caregivers to gender-expansive children, we have better reason than many to participate in this exchange. As allies and activists, we may discover that we're compelled to.

CHAPTER 11

LIVING AS AN ALLY

There are few places more sacred than the site where the bond of trust is held between an adult and a child. The nature of this bond isn't static, because both adult and child are always in a process of change, separately and together. So the bond, in one sense, is always being re-created. Safeguarding its integrity is our commitment to the children in our lives whom we love. I believe your bond, with your gender-expansive child, has compelled you to travel through the pages of this book. Significantly, to own your prejudice, examine your language, withdraw your allegiance and proactively change your position. Then, to turn outwards, 'spend time with difference' and explore community. The arc of your education, and your deep engagement with it, means that you're living as an ally already. What follows are some reflections on why, and how, to consolidate this.

Why continuing to learn matters...

To live as an ally means to enrol into an apprenticeship that may well last a lifetime. Happily for us, there's now an abundance of information and guidance to assist us in our training. Consequently, our individual learning can radiate in diverse ways, in keeping with the cross-fertilisation that has nourished our mind and spirit. Follow the internal prompts that pique your attention. Allow your specific needs, interests and energy to lead you, and choose material that 'touches' you. This is important. Please note carefully that the 'T' word I've used here is 'touch', not 'terrify'. Aim to monitor the information you're taking in, without slipping into avoidance and denial.[1] We know when we've been touched by something because our heart is involved in the process. We're learning beyond the intellect. When our emotions are included in our learning, then our humanity is also.

I've been enriched and, at times, heartbroken, by developing a deeper understanding of the journeys, experiences and challenges that transgender and gender-expansive children, youth and adults encounter. As Ruby's grandmother, I, like you, don't have the luxury of emotional distance from this material. Over the many months of my research, interactions, personal insights and writing, there have been times when I've had to put things down for a few days, to take a breath and allow my distressed gaze to rest elsewhere for a short while; then to collect my little ones from school, to dawdle together on the way home looking for butterflies, or to look up into the blossoming cherry trees above their small heads. I've finally come to understand that my 'health' as an ally depends on supporting myself effectively, in tandem with supporting others.

I have profound appreciation for the stories of those people who can't 'put things down' for a few days, because there isn't anywhere to 'put' the difference that society objects to in their body. As someone who is one step removed from this, 'taking a breath' is an outcome of my privilege. The generosity of many of the resources I've come across has humbled me. *Redefining Realness,* Janet Mock's memoir of how it is to grow up as a poor person of colour who is dual heritage and a trans woman, is one such example. As she states in her Introduction:

---

1   There's a lot of negative material available, online especially, and some of it is hateful. If you're engaging with it, please regularly take stock to ascertain whether your reasons for doing so are worth it in terms of any benefits for you and your family.

I believe that telling our stories, first to ourselves and then to one another and the world, is a revolutionary act. It is an act that can be met with hostility, exclusion, and violence. It can also lead to love, understanding, transcendence and community.[2]

Ms Mock's thoughtful and raw account of how the multiple intersecting identities she embodies have impacted on her life also exposes her to fire from several potential directions: classism, racism, sexism and transphobia. Each one, as we know, is a distinct cultural bully that conspires with all the others to create suffering. In this context, her courage is undeniable. I hadn't heard of Janet Mock until I asked a trans woman, who was delivering some training I was attending, if there was one 'story' she could recommend I read. Her signpost could not have directed me more accurately. *Redefining Realness* provided me with a masterclass in awareness. I've yet to graduate from it.

Then, just this week, a friend sent me the link to the French film *Tomboy*.[3] It's a 'quiet' film that captures, in nuanced and sensitive ways, the perspective of gender expansive Laure, who spends a summer going along with the assumption of children in her new neighbourhood that she's 'Mikael'. It's also a homage to the role loving sibling relationships can play in safeguarding self-worth, as six-year-old Jeanne, Laure's sister, demonstrates. The value of films such as this one is twofold. First, it gives expression to that which has been hidden or ignored, which means it can now be 'found'; and second, films such as *Tomboy* have the power to transport us back to childhood and adolescence – to re-ignite in us, as adults, what it feels like to be on these consecutive thresholds, and to have no idea at all what it is that's coming towards us. We only make the physical transition from child to adolescence once, and the emotional

2   Mock, J. (2014) *Redefining Realness: My Path to Womanhood*. New York, NY: Atria Books, p.xviii.
3   Sciamma, C. (2011) *Tomboy*. France: Hold Up Films.

and psychological safety net we depended on was solidarity with our peers. Our kids must encounter this developmental stage, but from a position of difference, not sameness, compounded by confusion. As one young person, reflecting back on her distraught 12-year-old self told me, 'I couldn't tell anyone because I didn't know what it was.'

There are many organisations that can assist our ongoing process of learning and transformation as an ally. Some are dedicated entirely to issues that are relevant to our children, and others act as part of their broader vision for a fair and inclusive society. As allies, we need to be equipped with facts, statistics and information to counterbalance the myths and misinformation about LGBTQ people in society. Remember that the sources of discrimination against all these communities are related and rooted in rejection of anyone who doesn't conform to the gender binary, so what we learn about one will inform us about the others.[4] Making it our business to generate conscious conversations, spread accurate information and neutralise negativity is valuable work. Not only will it expose barriers to equality that other people are unable to see, but doing so also contributes to dismantling them. The more we put our education into practice, the more embedded it will become. The more we learn, the more we'll be equipped to notice the gaps. The more we act, the weaker the Matrix will become. As one father reflected back to me:

> It's easy to ignore something when you're not involved in it, isn't it?
> I can keep my distance. You can be comfortably distant. It doesn't

---

4   Alongside LGBTQ people, trans and cisgender women are routinely subject to misogynistic and denigrating behaviour to keep them 'in line'. Recently, the front page of the UK's popular conservative tabloid newspaper the *Daily Mail* showed the Prime Minister, Teresa May, and the First Minister of Scotland, Nicola Sturgeon, sitting next to each other in a relaxed pose. A sexist caption accompanied it, disguised as 'cheeky banter': 'Never mind Brexit, who won Legs-it!' The message: 'You may head up two governments, but you're still women and you're still inferior.' Under the rules of the Matrix, this gives us the right to disrespect your professional roles, mock your intelligence and reduce you to your body parts.

help does it? It's the opposite to being an ally to someone. It's that 'ignorance is bliss'. That's exactly where I was.

For myself, I now realise that, as a cisgender white person, I'm no more exempt from the issue of transphobia than I am from the issue of racism. If Ruby's felt sense of gender had matched with her assigned one, I may never have learnt this truth about myself. I may never have contributed anything other than ignorance to the cause of children like her. I now understand how 'cis-ness' goes unnoticed in the way that whiteness does too.

The knowledge, awareness and experience I have, especially that which I've reflected on in depth, positions me powerfully as an ally. I'm an 'insider' who advocates for 'outsiders' from within my own group. A word of warning here, though, for all of us: Allies are not experts on the people or groups we align ourselves with, even if others want to portray us in this way.[5] Our role is to learn how to become a witness, and a supporter. We mustn't become deluded or seduced into thinking we're a specialist or an interpreter. As we know, our own personal stories have codified our experience of the world. And the privilege and rank we enjoy, arising out of the groups we belong to, shape and justify it. Re-mapping our worldview to include the perspectives of marginalised others is honourable, long-term work. When we commit to seeking out and absorbing the stories of gender-expansive and transgender people, we'll remain grounded in it. And the Four Keys – listening, imagination, empathy and courage – will unlock every gate along the way. Our kids, and other gender-diverse children, are at hand to help us with this. They are the

---

5   This point was made explicit to me by a trans woman I was having coffee with. I'm grateful to her for the insight. I was using the term 'ally' about myself and she advised me that, with the publication of the book, 'they'll make you into an expert' – meaning, as a cisgender person, in a cisgender culture, I'll be appointed more credibility to talk about being gender expansive, non-binary or trans, than a person who has direct experience and knowledge of being so.

pioneers openly occupying the verge of this emerging world – a world, finally, that is now being given a measure of public space.

Why being visible matters...

Let's take our minds back to Chapter 1, where I describe allies who are concerned with social justice as 'people who align themselves with a person who's been pushed to the edge of a group, or with a group that's been pushed to the edges of society'. For that person, or those groups, our visibility as allies is essential. How will they recognise or find us if we don't make ourselves known? When we abandon this work to people in non-mainstream groups to do for themselves, we're detracting energy from a budget that may already be drained. For many of them, routine risk-assessing in the majority of their social situations is enough. It would be enough for any of us, I imagine. If kids are left to work out who the allies are in their lives, they are in grave peril. As child-inclusive parents and caregivers, this list should be at our fingertips and we should know the phone number of everyone on it.

The more people our children can trust in each of the circles they move in, the safer they will be. Ann Masten, Professor in Child Development, believes that resilience doesn't only reside inside a child, rather it's distributed in the healthy, loving relationships with the people who make up that child's world. She describes this as 'ordinary magic'. Building resilience in our child means making sure the systems or circles they're moving in have an abundance of this.[6] Linda Reese, an attentive, and strikingly open woman from the north of England, shared with me how the 'ordinary magic' of one teacher turned everything around for her child in the space of one school

---

6   Masten, A. (2014) *Ordinary Magic: Resilience in Development*. New York, NY: Guilford Press.

year. Linda has three children and Lou, her youngest is a bubbly gender-expansive six-year-old with a very big smile:

> In the beginning the school weren't on board at all. They told us, 'Children need boundaries and you need to make sure that you steer Lou as [to] what clothes to wear. He needs to come to school dressed as a boy, so he doesn't get picked on in the playground.' But Lou's class teacher was amazing. He was on board from the beginning. Like one morning Lou had put *My Princess Boy*[7] in her bag. I didn't know until we got to school when he took it out to show Mr Jaimes. Do you know what he did? He said, 'Lou, can I read this book to the class at story time today?' Lou grew about two inches in two seconds! Then, without me asking him to, he took the book into the staff room and started a conversation about it there, and he took it into the playground and went through it with all the staff there too. He didn't have to do all this. I didn't know about it 'til later. We have a friend who's a governor at the school and she told us about it. We were so grateful to Mr Jaimes. In the end, everyone came full circle. Even the parish priest supported us.

Visibility matters. When we're brave enough to 'declare ourselves' in whatever capacity as an ally, it gives people around us permission to do so too. It incites courage in the hearts of others. We can model permission, and 'safety signal' in many ways: displaying a rainbow logo, which is a well-recognised symbol in LGBTQ communities, using inclusive language, approaching our child's school and enquiring about their equality policies, or speaking out when a non-mainstream person is the butt of a 'joke'. It's an arresting thing to watch a person from a mainstream group defending someone from a targeted group, especially in their presence. It confounds people. This isn't what we

---

7   Kilodans, C. and DeSimone, S. (2011) *My Princess Boy.* New York: Aladdin.

expect to happen, and it isn't commonplace either. In doing so, the ally is purposely drawing the line of fire in their direction. I'm not inferring that we should set out to do this; I am implying that it's an option we should always consider. It doesn't matter if our knees are weak when we do so, or adrenaline is spiking through our veins. This is all the more reason to honour our deeper self, the one that's stepping into the fray.

Being visible in these sorts of ways is a critical staging post in our life as an ally. It magnifies our values and makes concrete our commitment. In doing so it shows that our support isn't provisional, and that we'll stand up for others, even when they're unable to defend themselves.

Lewis, who we've met before, is a paramedic in a busy inner-city team. As he and I talked, he told me how his self-awareness, perceptions and activism have developed as a result of parenting Andi, his gender-expansive child:

> We went to an unconscious female, under a caravan. Everyone was working and I guess, because I'm hypersensitive to it, I realised she was transgender about five minutes before everyone else, before we had to cut this person's clothes off. So I said, 'We'll do it in the ambulance, not in the street.' And then you could see it dawning on the other paramedics, and someone said something like, 'Oh, look.' Not in a bad way, just like, 'I wasn't expecting that.' I snapped, 'It doesn't matter at all does it?' And everyone looked at me. Then I said, 'Let's just look after this person, shall we?'

CHAPTER 12

TRUSTING THE FUTURE

The world is changing. It always has. Nothing stands still, and gender is no exception. The Gender Matrix, constructed on the binary, is beginning to crumble. The rock face that gave rise to it has, all along, been shape-shifting, as wave after wave of activism has been washing up against it. Now a new gender landscape is emerging. We have good reason to trust in the future. When the cultural tectonic plates shifted in the 1960s, the existing template of gender fell between them. This created new freedoms for many people who, previously, had been denied them. Then, like now, young people are leading the way. This is their right, and they do so in the footsteps of others. More than any other reason, this is what gives me hope for what lays ahead of us. Phil, my son-in-law, asked me the other day, 'Anna, where are the positive stories? The ones that tell us this is a new expression of humanity?' Last week a friend called me and described how appalled her 12-year-old daughter was to be given a form in school that asked her to identify her gender as male or female. She had crossed out the word 'gender' and replaced it with 'sex'. 'That's what they really mean,' she indignantly told her mum, 'so they should say so.' Young people are doing it for themselves, they're not waiting for us to catch up. The world is changing. Then I heard about an introverted, shy 14-year-old cisgender boy who chose to do a presentation to the whole of his secondary school in support of his transgender peers. He sent me an email explaining why:

My tutor group, sitting in a diverse school where self-expression was encouraged, fell silent as we read Leelah's heartbreaking suicide note, including the sentences: 'My death needs to mean something. My death needs to be counted in the number of transgender people who commit suicide this year. I want someone to look at that number and say "that's fucked up" and fix it. Fix society. Please.' It made me feel numb. I couldn't believe that a child could be so misunderstood, controlled and made to feel so alone by their family, school and society – places that are supposed to protect children and nurture their growth – just because the gender wired into their brains and identities did not match the body that they had been born into. How on earth could that cause anybody any kind of harm? I thought of a brave friend in my year group, who had been the first student I know of in my school, to come out as openly transgender. Facing a lot of confusion and mocking, but also opening the door to so many other trans students at my school who have since come out, and in doing so, have helped to familiarise transgenderism as a gender identity within my school community. I thought of my friend and decided that Leelah Alcorn's death meant something to me.

Our assembly may not have made a huge change in my school, but what felt important was to make sure that no young person struggling with their gender identity felt isolated as Leelah had towards the end of her life – we wanted to share her message and her hope of real change in the way that society chooses to view and treat transgender people. No more ignorance and isolation, but love, acceptance and understanding. I remember thinking of my brave friend in the audience and hoping that our speaking out might help him.

Does this email inspire you? It did me. Does it give you grounds for hope? It has me. The world is changing. A generation of young people are viewing gender as a circle that has a place in it for everyone, and they believe that everyone in it holds a piece of the truth. The truth, as ever, isn't straightforward, harmonious and easy to arrive at, because truth is different for each one of us. But an emergent truth, one that is being called for in these times, is swelling into the mainstream. Consensus reality will follow suit.

The fact is, when Ruby's friends run naked around the garden with her and think nothing of it, it's a positive story. When people in her community use the right pronouns and correct other adults if they forget to, it's a positive story. When Ruby's access to the girls' bathroom is unquestioned in her school, it's a positive story. When her 86-year-old great grandmother takes Ruby in her arms and calls her 'my girl' it's a positive story. We must tell these positive stories because they need to be heard. Phil and Jude need to hear them, I need to hear them, you need to hear them, and parents and caregivers who are unsure and afraid need to hear them. Yes, the other stories, the ones that wake us up at night will still haunt us, and we must remember this is not the only story. Our children's prosperity depends on it.

Kristina Olson, Assistant Professor of Psychology at the University of Washington, is researching identity in a landmark study of 73 children aged 5–12 years, who are transgender.[1] What makes Olson's work exceptional is that all the children are living fully as their identified gender *and* in supportive environments. The Golden Thread has been woven into their families and circle of allies. The indicators, thus far, are unanimously positive, with no higher rates of depression than in the two control groups. Anxiety levels were slightly higher than the national norm, though not enough to create concern. Professor Olson witnessed the trials of a close friend with a transgender child who could barely find any scientific data to guide

1   Olson, K. R., Durwood, L., DeMeules, M. and McLaughlin, K. A. (2016) 'Mental health of transgender children who are supported in their identities.' *Pediatrics 137* (3) 2015–3223.

her as a parent. Olson's research was born out of this concern and is believed to be the first of its kind to look at the mental health of young children who have 'socially transitioned' in a supportive context.[2] Especially striking to Olson are the 'notable lower rates' of children internalising 'there's something's wrong with me' in homes where they've been facilitated to socially transition, compared to children who haven't. This, she believes, is evidence that a transgender child can be as happy and healthy as any other child. In 2017, a second study, including a focus on self-worth, corroborated these findings.[3]

Research such as this – and there is more emerging from other quarters[4] – is changing the cultural stories we've all been steeped in. Consensus reality is now beginning to reflect this. On 29 September 2016, this statement was released:

> Today, HRC Foundation joined with the American Academy of Paediatrics (AAP) and the American College of Osteopathic Paediatricians (ACOP), which together represent more than 66,000 paediatricians and paediatric specialists across the country, to release *Supporting and Caring for Transgender Children,* a new guide for community members and allies to ensure that transgender young people are affirmed, respected, and able to thrive.[5]

---

2   Bach, D. (2016) 'Transgender children supported in their identities show positive mental health.' *UW Today,* February 2016.

3   Durwood, L., McLaughlin, K. A. and Olson, K. R. (2017) 'Mental health and self-worth in socially transitioned transgender youth.' *Journal of the American Academy of Child and Adolescent Psychiatry 56,* 116–23.

4   Olson, K., Key, A. and Eaton, N. R. 'Gender cognition in transgender children.' *Psychological Science 26*(4) 467–74. de Vries, A. L. C., McGuire, J. K., Steensma, D. T., Wagenaar, E. C. F., Doreleijers, T. A. H. and Cohen-Kettenis, P. T. (2014) 'Young adult psychological outcome after puberty suppression and gender reassignment.' *Pediatrics 134*(4) 696–704.

5   McBride, S. (2016) 'HRC joins with nation's leading pediatric organizations on new guide supporting transgender youth.' Available at www.hrc.org/blog/hrc-joins-with-nations-pediatric-organizations-on-new-guide, accessed on 08 September 2017.

Let me repeat that: *'to ensure that transgender young people are affirmed, respected and able to thrive'.* In England, Ofsted, which inspects and regulates services for children and young people, states categorically in its 2015 guidance that it will now assess whether the rights of sexual minority and transgender children are being upheld across the country. The world is changing.

Knowledge means nothing if we fail to allow it to work on us. This morning I woke up with Ruby lying next to me. The window blind was half open and I watched my little one as she began to wriggle into the new day. I thought about the words of the transgender artist Anohni, which I'd read the evening before:

> What an incredible impulse that compels a five year old child to tell its parents it (gender) isn't what they think it is. Given just a tiny bit of oxygen, those children can flourish and be such a gift. They give other people licence to explore themselves more deeply, allowing the colours in their own psyche to flourish.[6]

My grandchild's small fierce journey across this landscape has taken me with her. When I challenged myself to redefine my own reality, in the light of hers, I didn't know significant aspects of my identity would be called into question. I assumed they didn't need to be. I was misguided in this. As I've held onto my grandchild's hand, beliefs that I was once attached to have been shed along the way: that gender identity and sex are interchangeable, that gender is binary, that gender equality is only two-dimensional. Consequently, the internal filigree that I perceive the world through has been reconfigured. My entitlement and unconscious privilege and rank as a cisgender woman have materialised before me. I am a better person because of this – less judgemental, more curious, less afraid of difference and more respectful towards it. I've begun to struggle out of a suffocating

---

6 *The Guardian Guide*, Saturday 9 April, 2016, p.9.

box that has been limiting my humanity. The radical innocence of Ruby offered me this gift of liberation.

As parents, caregivers and other allies, our visibility alone is creating social transformation. And we are everywhere, whispering, telling or singing a new story. It is not an uncomplicated one. It's riven through with mystery. There are no guarantees, and the uncertainties – medically, socially and psychologically – are profound. The potentiality for human well-being, health and happiness is immense; the opportunity to create a fairer world is breathtaking. When I became a grandmother, on the night of a full moon, these horizons were invisible to me. The Gender Matrix had obscured them. This is no longer the case, as I trust it isn't for you? The journey we've committed to take continues. All of us have travelled far, and together we shall travel further.

RESOURCES

Support, advice and activities

All About Trans
A dedicated project changing the media representation of trans people, 'one relationship at a time': www.allabouttrans.org.uk/about

Community Toolbox
A great resource to engage, work with and build community: ctb.ku.edu/en

Gender Spectrum
A comprehensive website dedicated to creating sensitive and inclusive gender environments, with multiple resources on offer: www. genderspectrum.org

Global Action for Trans Equality (GATE)
GATE's mission is to work internationally on gender identity, gender expression and bodily issues. It's a human rights organisation with an explicit potential mandate: https://transactivists.org

Perception testing
How to explore and uncover our perceptions and 'selective thinking':
www.princeton.edu/~hammett/puzzles

Straight for Equality (PFLAG National)
Guide to Being a Trans Ally: https://bolt.straightforequality.org/files/
Straight%20for%20Equality%20Publications/2.guide-to-being-a-trans-
ally.pdf

Understanding Prejudice
An excellent resource that includes a number of interactive activities,
including Implicit Assumption Tests: www.understandingprejudice.org

United Kingdom

Support for parents and caregivers

Gendered Intelligence
www.genderedintelligence.co.uk

The Gender Identity Research and Education Society (GIRES)
www.gires.org.uk

Mermaids: Embrace. Empower. Educate
www.mermaidsuk.org.uk

Scottish Transgender Alliance
www.scottishtrans.org

Transgender Equality Network Ireland
www.teni.ie

Information for schools

Intercom Trust
Schools Transgender Guidance (in partnership with Devon and Cornwall Police and Cornwall Council): www.intercomtrust.org.uk/item/55-schools-transgender-guidance-july-2015

Schools OUT UK
Transgender Guidance for Wrexham Schools 2015: www.schools-out.org.uk/wp-content/files_mf/1470607662TransGenderGuidanceSchoolsFinal.pdf

Stonewall
An Introduction to Supporting LGBT Young People: A Guide for Schools: http://www.stonewall.org.uk/sites/default/files/an_introduction_to_supporting_lgbt_young_people_-_a_guide_for_schools_2015.pdf'

United States

Support for parent and caregivers

Family Acceptance Project
https://familyproject.sfsu.edu

GLAAD
www.glaad.org/transgender

Human Rights Campaign
Finding Support for You and Your Family: www.hrc.org/resources/transgender-children-and-youth-finding-support-for-you-and-your-family

The Trevor Project
www.thetrevorproject.org

Information for schools

Education Week
Having Allies Makes a Difference: www.edweek.org/ew/collections/
pdk/2013/02/14/kappan_pardini.html

Gender Spectrum
Schools in Transition: www.genderspectrum.org/staging/wp-content/
uploads/2016/06/Schools_In_Transition_6.3.16.pdf

GLSEN: Gay, Lesbian and Straight Education Network
Report: Trans Youth & Schools Facilities: www.glsen.org/article/new-
report-details-extensive-harms-denying-transgender-students-access-
school-facilities

ACKNOWLEDGEMENTS

To all the gender-expansive young people, their families, friends and allies, who shared your stories with me, I am indebted to you. Your willingness to offer them to me, a stranger, humbled, educated and changed my way of being in the world.

To my daughter and son-in-law: I honour the depth of your courage and your open hearts. I honour your compassion and capacity to live gracefully with the unknown. I honour your refusal to be anything other than true to your calling as parents.

To my sons, each one of you brings a different quality and light to my life. Thank you, and your wonderful partners, for sustaining me with love, laughter and unending support.

To Mike, for blessing our children with solid ground to stand on, grow from and always to return to.

To my mum, sisters and their families: thank you for loving my daughter, and her daughter, unconditionally. This is a gift without measure.

To the 'Y family': My gratitude is unbounded that it was your family, specifically, who were chosen to walk this path alongside mine.

To my inner circle of friends: how could I have accomplished this without you? The phone calls, meal stops, cheerleading texts and steady companionship when writing, research and responsibilities felt 'too much'. Thank you.

Anita MacCallum and Luke Nickel, writing comrades, gratitude for stepping into my life when you did.

I am deeply appreciative of the network of new contacts both in the US and the UK, who supported this endeavour so generously. In particular, Brock Dumville, Berkeley Wilde and Henry Poultney.

Many, many hands have joined together from different places and points in my life to help create this book. I am grateful for every touch. No matter the intention, each one has contributed to the whole.

INDEX

acceptance 168–70
accountability 33
acculturation 67–70
'acting as if…' technique 192–3
active enquiry 135–7
activism 216–8
Adewunmi, B. 7
Adkins, D. 148
adult, supportive 28–9
Africa, LGBTQ rights in 59, 60
agency 129–30
Alaers, J. 56, 57
Alexander, D. 78
allegiance
    acknowledging 153–5
    withdrawing from Matrix 168–72
    see also beliefs
Allen, J. 207
Allport, Gordon 200
ally
    characteristics of an 32–4
    identity as an 27
    path of an 14–5
Amnesty International 59, 60
animated films 77–8
Anohni 235
Assagioli, A. 152
assignment of gender 40, 70–1
assumptions 157
attachment 63–6

attention-intention-action strategy 185,
    190–1
attunement 63, 92–4
authoritative parenting 34
avoidance 132

Bach, D. 234
Baird, V. 44, 56
Baldwin, J. 132
Baptise, N. 59
beliefs
    and behaviour 172–7
    changing 159–63
    confronting 155–6
    identifying 156–9
    see also allegiance
belonging 219
bias 12, 80–3
    see also discrimination; Gender Matrix;
        prejudice
Blake, William 46
Bloom, B. 170
Boeskool, Chris 102
Bombastic magazine 59
Brill, S. 42, 165, 166, 167, 168
bullying 109–10

Cairns, K. 63, 64
career choices 75
cartoons 77–8
celebration 221–2